I'M SORRY I HAVEN'T A CLUE

The Best of Forty Years

3 5 7 9 10 8 6 4

Windmill Books
20 Vauxhall Bridge Road
London SW1V 2SA

Windmill Books is part of the Penguin Random House group of companies whose addresses
can be found at global.penguinrandomhouse.com.

First published by Preface Publishing in 2012

First published in paperback by Windmill Books in 2015

www.windmill-books.co.uk

A CIP catalogue record for this book is available from the British Library.

ISBN 9780099510543

Printed and bound by Clays Ltd, St Ives PLC

MIX
Paper from
responsible sources
FSC® C018179

Penguin Random House is committed to a sustainable
future for our business, our readers and our planet.
This book is made from Forest Stewardship
Council® certified paper.

I'M SORRY I HAVEN'T A CLUE

The Best of Forty Years

GRAEME GARDEN, TIM BROOKE-TAYLOR, BARRY CRYER,
WILLIE RUSHTON, IAIN PATTINSON AND JEREMY HARDY

EDITED AND COMPILED BY JON NAISMITH

DESIGNED BY NEAL TOWNSEND

WITH SPECIAL THANKS TO BETHAN BIDE

 WINDMILL BOOKS

CONTENTS

FOREWORD *by* STEPHEN FRY

I CAN'T remember the time I saw my first episode of *Have You a Clue That You Are Being Served?* but I do recall that the experience struck me amidships like a U-boat torpedo breaching the hull of a naval corvette. It is safe to say that I was never the same again.

Barry Cryer's wickedly observed pussy-flaunting Mrs Slocombe and Tim Brooke-Taylor's saucy and highly eroticised Miss Brahms made a formidable pair (and possessed one!), pitted as they were against the wicked charm of Willie Rushton's grumpy but endearing Mr Grainger, Graeme Garden's flamboyant, cheeky, but never unnecessary or inappropriate Mr Humphries and Colin Sell's wise-cracking Mr Lucas. All presided over with aplomb by the dashing, debonair and unflappable Captain Peacock, whose striped trousers and scarlet carnation seemed to crystallise everything we mean when we say 'British'.

With their catch phrases, 'You'll have had your I'm free!', 'It'll ride up Mornington Crescent' and 'Bring me the head of merchandising', this team of seasoned variety retirees transmitted their quick wit and inimitable sense of the absurd to generation after generation of radio viewers the world over.

HYACTYABS has run now for seventy-five years, and a new generation of indentured newbies has been added to the roster of dentured veterans who began it all. I myself have had the honour of guesting on the show more than once, my pleasing bass-baritone bringing joy to Colin's musical heart. Jack Dee has taken on the mantle of Captain Peacock, and Sandi Toksvig, Paul Merton, Tony Hawks, Ross Noble, Andy Hamilton, Jeremy Hardy and many other foul-mouthed young louts have carried on the great tradition of this perennial favourite, hauling it reluctantly into this so-called modern era of high definition smart-faxes and 3D puns.

It would be wrong not to mention the marvellous contribution of twinkly Jon Naismith as Young Mr Grace and Iain Pattinson as jug-eared managerial ass Mr Rumbold. Without their benign control the good ship *I'm Sorry I'll Serve You Again* might well have foundered on the rocks of ribaldry or found itself stranded on the sandbanks of non-compliance.

With tears of mirth rolling down the deeply trenched lines of my own now aged and withered countenance I raise a glass of tonic wine to another seventy-five years of amiable high-jinks from a comedy team who can rightly be said to have put the 'great' in BBC.

Stephen Fry.

Famous First Words

Where the teams are invited to suggest the first words of people either still living, or appearing on 'I'm a Celebrity Get Me Out of Here'...

'I'll be back'
Oedipus

'Boo!'
Alfred Hitchcock

'My Mum's got four nipples'
Jeffrey Archer

'Da Doo Doo Doo Da Da Da Da'
Sting

'Just try smacking me'
Vinnie Jones

'When do I get the teeth?'
Janet Street-Porter

'Oh, thanks for nothing'
Philip Larkin

'What a forceps saga!'
John Galsworthy

'Knees up Mother Brown'
Chas & Dave

'Where are the other two cords?'
Rick Parfitt of Status Quo

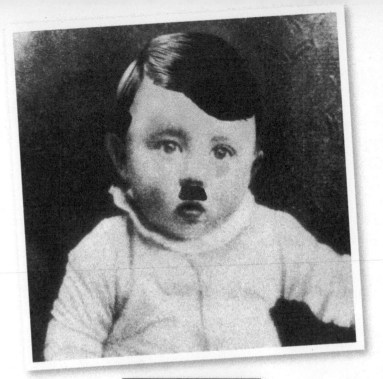

'This isn't Poland'

Adolf Hitler

'I'm always going to look like this'
William Hague

'Over here!'
Colonel Tom Thumb

'Hello, good evening and talcum'
Sir David Frost

'Sorry, wrong planet'
John Redwood

'Never again'
Julian Clary

'Surely there must be a better way than this'
Mary Whitehouse

'Da-daaaa!'
Harry Houdini

'I'll break the waters if you don't mind'
Charlton Heston

'Cut! I'd like to go again, love. Lots more screaming this time'
Michael Winner

'Go ahead, punk. Cut my cord'
Clint Eastwood

'As I was saying'
The Dalai Lama

'Da-Da! entered the room, his manly shoulders silhouetted in the doorway...'
Barbara Cartland

'No nurse, that's not the umbilical cord'
Tom Jones

'Why is everyone screaming?'
Michael Gove

'Those dirty nappies give me a great idea!'
Mr McDonald, the hamburger king

'I'm out! Everybody out!'
Arthur Scargill

'D'you know, this is the first time I've seen Ma's'
Patrick Moore

'Goo goo. Oh, repetition of goo'
Clement Freud

'And tell me, have you been doing this job for long?'
The Queen (to midwife)

'Goo Goo Gaa Gaa, Boo Bop A Loo Ma'
Little Richard

'I think you'll like what I've done in there'
Laurence Llewelyn-Bowen

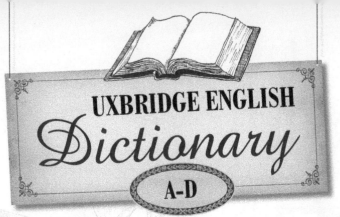

UXBRIDGE ENGLISH
Dictionary
A-D

Alcopops
Alcoholic dads

Apocalypse
Disastrous collagen injection

Arsenal
The whole body

Article
Tease a pirate

Asterisk
The chances of being hit by an asteroid

Fig.1. *Arsenal*

Affiliation
Affair with a horse

Agog
Half-finished Jewish temple

Bazaar
Barry the pirate

Fig.2. Catastrophe

Candid
Past tense of can do

Cardiology
The study of knitwear

Catastrophe
My moggie has won a prize

Catchphrase
Howzat!

Caustic
Good heavens, a twig

Celery
A bit like a cellar

Claptrap
A condom

Clematis
Not quite what you're trying to find

Crucifix
Religious adhesive

Bidet
Two days before D-Day

Bling
The sound of a Chinese telephone

Bombardier
An overly aggressive form of culling

Brocade
Medical assistance for badgers

Fig.3. Brocade

Dependable
A confident swimmer

Descent
To remove the smell

Detonation
Greece

Disdain
To insult a Scandinavian

Doodah
A cool pirate

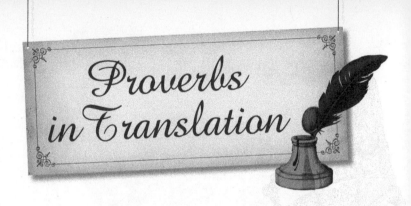

Proverbs in Translation

Proverbs provide an essential life code, but many need updating. Whilst it's still true that you can't make a silk purse out of a pig's ear, there's nothing to stop you making a pork pie. And it's not the broth that's spoilt by too many cooks, but the TV schedule. Now that the English language is spoken in every corner of the globe, it's high time to translate some proverbs to make them useful to foreigners and to ignore the fact that globes don't have corners.

AUSTRALIA

Red sky at night shepherd's delight. Red sky in the morning your sheep are on fire

Love is blind, so brace yourself Sheila

CANADA

A rolling stone gathers no moose

CHINA

Two Wongs make a Wong

FRANCE

Don't teach your grandmother
to suck existentialists

One man's meat is another
man's poisson

GERMANY

Brevity is the soul of wit –
have you noticed how long our
words are?

Laughter is the best medicine,
but unfortunately it's not
available on prescription

Early to bed, early to rise,
makes a man healthy, wealthy
and more likely to get a sun
lounger

HOLLAND

If the cap fits, you're safe

INDIA

Do wash your dirty linen in
public

JAPAN

All work and no play makes us
a booming economic nation

Get rid of the scavenging
birds before you bring the
harvest in (or `rook before you
reap')

KOREA

Brevity is the Seoul of wit

MIDDLE EAST

If you can't beat 'em, chop
their hands off

NORWAY

A nod is as good as a wink to a
blind Norse

ROME

Milton Keynes was built in a
day

RUSSIA

Chernobyl: Two heads are
better than one

SCOTLAND

He who pays the piper will be
held personally responsible

In Aberdeen they say a fool
and his money are most
welcome

Cleanliness is next to Inverness

SPAIN

Give a man a fish and you feed
him for a day. Teach a man
to fish and he'll be off the
Cornish coast in no time

SUSSEX

Marry in Hastings, repent at
your leisure centre...

SWEDEN

One swallow doesn't make a
satisfying film

TAIWAN

Give a thief enough rope
and he'll start a successful
rope-making business

TURKEY

Better late than Greek

VENICE

Love me love my Doge

COMPLETE
Greetings Cards

PART 1

Barry Cryer was telling us that just before their Ruby
Wedding Anniversary, his wife discovered him signing
a card. It was dedicated to that special person he hasn't
missed a day away from in forty years, the first face he
sees in the morning and the last face he sees at night.
Who knew they did a special greetings card for the
landlord of the Dog and Duck?

ON BECOMING
GRANDPARENTS

An extension of your family,
Grandparents you've become. . .
~~Let's lift a glass and celebrate~~
~~The new life that's just begun~~
Or as they say in Middlesbrough
Well done – you're twenty-one

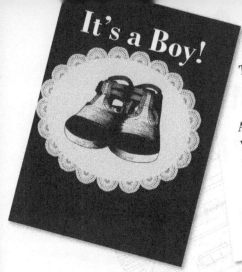

It's a Boy!

Hello there little fellow!
The good news going round
Is that you've made a
'happy landing'
And arrived all safe and sound
Well this just comes to tell you
That you're lucky as can be. . .
~~To become the newest member~~
~~Of so nice a family~~
You'll never have a sister
Thanks to my vasectomy

ON LEAVING COLLEGE

Your college graduation
Makes us very proud
We're shouting it from the rooftops
We're your parents – it's allowed
So go forth now with gusto
You've passed the schooling test. . .
~~We love you and we're proud of you~~
~~You deserve the very best~~
We've changed the locks, we've let your room
Goodbye you bloody pest

HAPPY 16th BIRTHDAY

Sixteen years have come and gone
And now your birthday's here. . .
~~We hope that all you wish for~~
~~Will be yours throughout the year~~
And you can now do legally
What you've been doing all bloody year

A FATHER'S DAY CARD

Dad, you are so loving and kind,
And often you know
What I have on my mind.
You're someone who listens,
Suggests, and defends
And dad you're one of
My very best friends.
You're proud of my triumphs,
But when things go wrong. . .
~~You're always so patient and~~
~~helpful and strong~~
You hit me

AN EASTER CARD

Guess who's hop, hop, hopping your way?
To wish you a hap, hap, happy holiday.
Loaded with goodies made just for you. . .
~~It's the Easter Bunny, that's who~~
It's the one-legged stammerer
from Number 2

AN ENGAGEMENT CARD

You are a perfect couple
Yes such a heavenly pair. . .
~~This brings a wish for happiness~~
~~In the future that you'll share~~
Why don't you get them out for us
And wave them in the air

Costcutters

PART 1

As the worldwide economic crisis marches on, gloom sweeps over the broadcasting industry, and ever more draconian cuts are being made to programme budgets. Barry Cryer actually raised funds by selling off some of his old clothes. And how grateful the makers of 'Downton Abbey' were to find authentic costumes. Here are some low-budget remakes of TV and radio shows.

'The National Pottery Live'

'No Deal'

'Harry Potter and the Paul Daniel's Magic Set'

'Slumdog Milliner'

'Darning on Ice'

'The Devil Wears Primark'

'Thomas the Tank Top'

'The Case Book of Eamonn Holmes'

'Dial M for Merthyr'

'Conan the Librarian'

'Star Truck'

'And Judy'

'Le Misérable'

'Oh! What a Lovely Disagreement'

E.M. Forster's *A Passage to Islington*

'High Wycombe Five-O'

'Seven Brides for Seven Quid'

'The Wizard of Oswestry'

'Ben Herpes'

'Third in Line to the Throne Kong'

'The Bourne Soup Recipe'

'Down and Out in Beverley Nichols'

Mozart's 'Così Fan One-te'

Gibbon's 'Decline and Fall of the Hackney Empire'

'Samson and a Lilo'

Chekhov's 'The Sister' and 'The Cherry Bowl'

'The Camomile Tea Bag'

'Annie Get Your Stick'

'Charlie and the Chocolate Biscuit'

'Joseph and his Amazing Beige Cardigan'

'Around the Block in Eighty Days'

'Alice in Poundland'

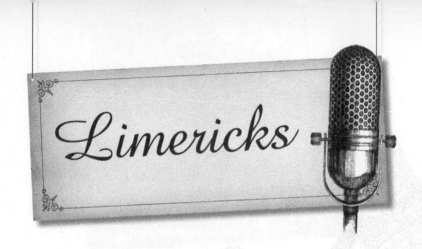

Limericks

The name Limerick is a corruption of the old French word for America – 'L'Amerique'. French migrants sailing to the New World were blown off course to Southern Ireland, where they landed and mistakenly called it 'L'Amerique'. There is still a large community of 'Limerick' French to this day, as visitors to their annual festival of sheep burning and lorry wrecking will testify.

Ben Kingsley, while dressed up as Ghandi
Went into a bar for a shandy
To wipe up the froth
He used his loin cloth
And the barmaid said, 'Blimey, that's handy!'

While pretending to read some Voltaire
Strange noises emerged from my chair
Then George Bernard Shaw
Said 'I'll open the door'
Thank God for a breath of fresh air!

I've a small breed of dog called a Scottie

Who's house trained and sits on a potty

He gives a loud yap

The mischievous chap

Then stands up and wipes his wee botty

My wife and I sadly are parting
In our lounge there's a farm she is starting
She's fed all the pigs
On syrup of figs
No wonder my eyes are still smarting

A cheeky young cowpoke called Hank
Went into the woods with a plank
For three or four winters
He suffered the splinters
But laughed all the way to the bank

There was a young lady called Chuck
(And we're all wishing Barry good luck!)
'Twas an old merchant banker
Who finally sank er
With a highly trained Muscovy Duck

In a pub with old Thomas Aquinas
I was rapidly struck by his shyness
When I said, 'It's your shout'
He quickly ran out
So that was a bit of a minus

Consuming too much herbal tea
Can cause havoc when having a pee
When out on the razzle
You tend to pass basil
And last night old Basil passed me!

In the shower I bumped into the Pope
He said, 'I have given up hope'
Then he lay in the aisle
With a faraway smile
While we hit him with soap-on-a-rope

As she swallowed her fifth jellied eel
Babs cried, 'Ooh I just love how they feel!'
But the sixth eel was limp
So she gobbled a shrimp
Now she stars in prawn movies in Deal

When Santa was out on his sleigh
He said, 'How I love Christmas Day!
All over the Earth
We rejoice in His birth.'
And the reindeer all shouted, 'Oy veh!'

TRAIL OF THE *Lonesome Pun*

PART 1

Cynics may suggest that the thinnest of programme premises are often wrung solely out of one simple piece of lazy punning wordplay after no more than a few minutes' thought, and this has been discussed on Radio 4's 'Thinking Allowed' programme. But the teams always prove them wrong when they play the game called: 'Trail of the Lonesome Pun'.

Nine o'clock tonight on Channel 5, 29-year-old Heather Wilson has to decide how to spend her hard-earned money. Is it to be a holiday in Monaco or the breast enhancement she's always promised herself? That's:
`Monte Carlo or Bust`

On Saturday at 2.30 p.m. we show highlights of the competition to find the world's finest bikini wax. That's:
`The Brazilian Grand Prix`

Wallis and Gromit

Tomorrow afternoon Her Majesty the Queen takes the salute as a division of the Household Cavalry are painted pale pink from head to toe by Prince Philip. That's:
`Colouring the Troop´

Coming up also, live bingo from a popular French shrine. That's:
`The House of Lourdes´

Tonight on Radio 4, a new programme following the careers of Liberal Democrat MPs. That's:
`The Weak in Westminster´

Ever wondered if a minor TV celebrity is descended from pirates? Then tune in to:
`Who Do You Think You Arrrrgh?´

This afternoon Tory Chairman Eric Pickles and Labour peer Lord Prescott bury their differences as they go sketching together, armed only with sketchbook and pencil in:
`An Oversize Pair of Drawers`

Later on this afternoon, how Scandinavians lose their hair trying to steal from a poorly protected furniture warehouse in:
`Locking the Table Store after the Norse has Moulted`

And next on Radio 4, a lot of horrible whining coming out of your radio speakers. Yes it's:
`Feedback`

And now on BBC4, a study of the human breast in our society, culture and art. A personal retrospective by Boris Johnson. That's:
`Arse About Tit`

Tonight on Sky1, a documentary examining the scarcity of public toilets for women with:
`Mind Your Pees and Queues`

Channel 4 presents an award-winning documentary about the late Mrs Simpson, Duchess of Windsor, and her life-long struggle with sea sickness. That's
`Wallis and Vomit`

Later tonight on BBC1, a tribute to stylist Gok Wan as his many friends and colleagues share their opinions of the man and his rise to fame. That's:
`Gok Wan King Style Guru`

Tonight on BBC2, Jamie Oliver looks at Britain's overweight population. Nine o'clock this evening:
`The Obesity Rollers`

And later on Radio 4, a new series in which bankers describe their feelings about the tax payer. That's:
`Up You and Yours`

In My Pants

Here's one you can play at home. All you have to do is to add the words '. . . in my pants' to any film, book or programme title.

Just a Minute
in my pants

Gone With the Wind
in my pants

Oranges Are Not the Only Fruit
in my pants

A River Runs Through It
in my pants

Finding Nemo
in my pants

Rear Window
in my pants

Hot Fuzz
in my pants

It Happened One Night
in my pants

The Princess and the Pea
in my pants

The Third Man
in my pants

The Sound of Music
in my pants

Don't Look Now
in my pants

The Battle of the Little Bighorn
in my pants

Who Do You Think You Are?
in my pants

Woman's Hour
in my pants

Waking the Dead
in my pants

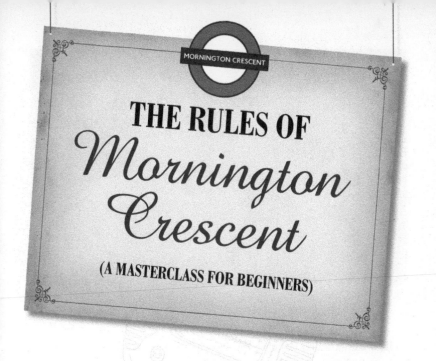

THE RULES OF
Mornington Crescent
(A MASTERCLASS FOR BEGINNERS)

It is safe to assume that even the most inexperienced beginner will have a sound working knowledge of the basic rules of the Straight Game, so we shall waste no time on them here.

THE BOARD AND PIECES

On opening the brightly but helpfully decorated box, you will find nestling inside it the Board, the Pieces and a Booklet. Tip them out on to a flat surface and familiarise yourself with them in the usual way.

* The Board has four edges: Topside, Rightbottom, Leftbottom and Wing. Arrange the Board so that Topside faces the Dealer, if there happens to be one present. The square playing surface is divided into a grid consisting of 83 identical squares. (As squares 66, 13, 47 and 49 are only used during Advanced Shunts, they are almost invariably ignored.)

* The six enamelled Bakelite Pieces are in the form of: 1 dachshund, 1 catapult, 1 bishop, 1 Aga oven and 2 potatoes. This is their correct order, unless Hopkins' Constrictions are applied. Each piece has a value of 0.27p.

* The Booklet contains hints on pronunciation, Appendix A, and a list of recommended snacks for the Long Game. In it you will also find a useful list of addresses from which replacement Booklets may be purchased.

Generally speaking, the Board, Pieces and Booklet will only serve to confuse the players and are best discarded at this stage. Please, as always, dispose of them thoughtfully, or at least pensively. Once they are out of the way. . .

YOU ARE READY TO PLAY MORNINGTON CRESCENT!

THE TEAMS

Each side consists of two to thirteen Teams of at least 1 player each.

The Captains (and Other Ranks): the Team Captain is selected by throwing a dice – whoever it hits is the chosen leader. The Captain then appoints the Lieutenants, Petty Officers, Senior Conductors and so forth. This depends, of course, on the size of the teams. For example, very short players make poor Sergeants. You will soon get the hang of this.

TERRITORIES

No Team of more than two players is allowed to declare Territories and this applies to Teams of two or fewer players as well.

CLOTHING

Clothing should be comfortable and smart, especially the skirt or trousers. It is important that sleeves and socks should not restrict gestures. Hats are permitted, but only one per head.

The Opening: once all players are in position according to the Constantine Deployment. . .

YOU ARE READY TO PLAY MORNINGTON CRESCENT!

THE END GAME

The so-called End Game begins with the first move. This sounds a great deal more complicated than it is. The first move, also known as the opening gambit, *le jeu d'engagement* or *das Erstschachtschlage*, is made by the player to the right of the Track-holder and play then progresses alternately to the right and left. Other players may of course interrupt this progression, but only in strict sequence. Incidentally, inexperienced players are often confused by the number of first moves available and find themselves dithering, which loses points. It is usually safe to begin with a blot above the Line and over the years Putney Bridge has proved to be a pretty solid banker.

Once the Primary has been enstaked and accepted, without prime challenge (McAwdle's), play continues *pet-a-pet* and only ends when one of the players is in a position to bag 'Mornington Crescent' itself. Play is then over. With these simple basics in mind. . .

YOU ARE READY TO PLAY MORNINGTON CRESCENT!

THE OFFSIDE RULE

There is no more hotly disputed yet widely misunderstood aspect of the Game than the Offside Rule. However, as 'Nosey' Parker (the Mornington Crescent Tipster of the 'Independent on Sunday') puts it so succinctly: 'If it weren't for the Offside Rule there would be nothing to prevent a player from declaring "Mornington Crescent" on his or her opening move! This would end the game at a stroke and might deprive the players of much of their fun.' For this reason alone, the Offside Rule is of importance and should be memorised:

Rule 77a. If a player moves to such a location that there are less than two occupied bases between the location played and the next but one Shift Zone, Morton's Convention being in play, whether the Loop has been vectored from either Diagonal or not, and all other players are out of Nip, then that move is declared 'under-struck' and therefore void, meaning that the player has no option but to offer a Bakerloo Redress and be declared out of line and must miss a turn.

SCORING

Devotees are proud of the fact that Mornington Crescent is the only game still played which has a Binary Scoring System. Those unfamiliar with the principles of Binary Arithmetic are advised to consult the excellent 'HM Customs & Excise Pamphlet 5867 – Arithmetic, Binary, Principles of' by Knoeppfler and Hoogstraaten (HMSO 7/6d). Applying a basic rule of thumb, the system can be summarised thus: the Winner scores 1. Everyone else scores 0.

SUMMARY

Well, there you have it. Simple really, isn't it? One final point: before embarking on a life-long and passionate devotion to the Great Game and pitting your wits against Crescenteers of experience and guile, ask yourself this question:

ARE YOU SURE YOU ARE READY TO PLAY MORNINGTON CRESCENT?

Texting for Pensioners

Isn't it terrible the way older listeners are patronised? I said: ISN'T IT TERRIBLE THE WAY OLDER LISTENERS ARE PATRONISED? With more mobile phones in Britain than people, text messages have become the preferred means of communication for millions. But text acronyms have so far been devised only for the young. What acronyms might prove popular with the older listener?

OMG
Oh Me Gout

TBC
To Be Cremated

MYOB
Make Your Own Bovril

WTF
Whoops Tiny Fart

BRB
Blue Rinse Babe

RNR
Rheumatic And Racist

OAP
On A Promise

NIMBY
Naughty In Me Breeches
Yesterday

WYSIWYG
What You See Is Where've You Gone?

BFF
Bedpan Frighteningly Full

RSVP
Really Serious Varicose Problem

IMHO
It's My Hip Operation

OBE
Oh Blooming `Eck

POV
Please Order Viagra

WYWH
Will You Want Horlicks?

ASAP
Asleep After Pill

ETA
Eighth Time of Asking

WTF
Wig Tilted Forward

POW
Peed On Me Wellingtons

MILF
Midnight I'm Likely To Fart

Barry found three bars on his mobile. What a great service that 'locate-a-pub' app provides

Quote... Unquote

This is the game where the panel are presented with the first half of memorable quotations to finish off. Advertisers spend their lives struggling to come up with quotable phrases, but many are destined never to catch the public imagination. The jingle employed by Quilley's Throat Lozenges was a prime example: 'When your throat is dry and sore, Go down to your chemist store, Don't you all be silly billies, Get fast relief when you suck Quilley's!'

Shall I compare thee to a summer's day, thou art. . .
bloody miserable

'Twas brillig, and the slithy toves did gyre and gimble in the wabe. . .
Yes never mind all that, sir, blow into this please

Do not go gentle into. . .
kickboxing

Miss Joan Hunter Dunn, Miss Joan Hunter Dunn. . .
paging Miss Joan Hunter Dunn

The owl and the pussycat went to sea in a beautiful pea green boat, they. . .
drowned

Do not stand at my grave and weep, I am not there. . .
I'm behind you

QUILLEY'S
SINCE 1865

When your throat
is dry and sore
Go down to your
chemists' store
Don't you all be silly billies
Get fast relief when
you suck Quilley's

150 LOZENGES

QUILLEY'S THROAT PASTILLES

It was a lover and his lass with a hey and a ho and. . .
another ho

Half a league, half a league, half a league. . .
paging Arthur League

Should old acquaintance be forgot and never brought to mind?. . .
Yes

And did those feet in ancient time walk upon England's mountains green?. . .
NO

Play it, Sam. Play. . .
the last movement of Shostakovich's 5th piano concerto in E minor and make it snappy

The best laid plans of mice and men. . .
seldom coincide

Of all the gin joints in all the towns in all the world, she walks into. . .
a lamppost

Frankly my dear, I don't give a. . .
discount

Et tu. . .
but couldn't manage three Shredded Wheat

We shall fight on the beaches, we shall fight on the landing grounds, we shall fight in the fields and in the streets, we shall fight in the hills, we shall never. . .
go near the Germans

Oh give me a home where the buffalo. . .
don't lie around on the sofa eating crisps

To be or not to be. . .
that is the apiarist's dilemma

Fifteen men on a dead man's chest. . .
I always thought rugby football was dangerous

It is a wise father that knows his own. . .
blood group

When shall we three meet again? In thunder, lightning or in. . .
Sainsbury's

Walls have ears. . .
but Lyons Maid has stripy bits

If you can keep your head when all about you are losing theirs. . .
you'll be taller than anybody else

It was a lover and his lass, with a. . .
large egg whisk

If God did not exist, it would be necessary to. . .
break it very gently to the Pope

The quality of mercy is not strained. . .
but I can recommend the cabbage

Mad dogs and Englishmen go. . .
woof woof! Bring back Maggie!

My love is like a red, red. . .
well see for yourself doctor

One small step for man. . .
a taxi ride for Ronnie Corbett

If Wales could be rolled out flat
as England, it would. . .
*be known as the Hereford
bypass*

Some chicken – some neck. . .
*some peas and some roast
potatoes*

Blow, winds, and crack your
cheeks. . .
*but for God's sake put the cat
out first*

The curfew tolls the knell of
parting day,
The lowing herd winds slowly
o'er the lea,
The ploughman homeward plods
his weary way. . .
*Thomas Gray, 'News at Ten',
Country Churchyard*

And all because the lady loves
milk. . .
men

You'll never be alone with a. . .
multiple personality disorder

Monsieur, with these Ferrero
Rocher you are really. . .
scraping the barrel

Alas poor Yorick, I knew. . .
he wasn't well at breakfast

Come home to a real. . .
bollocking

Eight out of ten people say their
cats. . .
*from the back look like pencil
sharpeners*

If you like a lot of chocolate on
your biscuit join. . .
the Euphemism Society

Lipsmackin' thirstquenchin' acetastin' motivatin' goodbuzzin' cooltalkin' highwalkin' fastlivin' evergivin' coolfizzin'. . .
You & Yours

The stain says hot, the label says. . .
don't believe the talking stain

You'll wonder where the yellow went when you. . .
wash the bedsheets

Go to work on an. . .
Widdecombe

Softness is a thing called. . .
erectile dysfunction

Don't you just love being in. . .
continent

Top breeders recommend. . .
shagging

You can't put a better bit of butter on your. . .
list of lubricants

A finger of fudge is just enough to. . .
get you on a register

Get back your 'Ohhh' with. . .
a finger of fudge

Do the shake and vac and. . .
leave the gents

Do you love someone enough to give them. . .
chlamydia

Oxo gives a meal. . .
tiny shards of foil

Between love and madness lies. . .
syphilis

Let the train take the. . .
piss

Genius is 2% inspiration and. . .
99% arithmetic

Only the crumbliest, flakiest. . .
people appear on 'I'm a Celebrity Get Me Out of Here'

They're tasty, tasty, very very tasty, they're. . .
too young for you, Tim

Plop plop, fizz fizz, oh what a. . .
holiday we had in India

The Delightful Samantha

For many years the teams have been more than happy to leave their points in the capable hands of the show's scorer, Samantha. Samantha has a wide range of interests, and sits on many boards and committees. The TUC even invited her to sit on its National Executive. . .

SAMANTHA ON DOGS

Samantha always tells us when it's time to let her whippet out. The little fellow scampers up to Samantha holding a couple of crackers out and pants around her ankles.

SAMANTHA ON ICE CREAM

Samantha regularly meets with an Italian gentleman friend who takes her out for an ice cream. She says she likes nothing better than to spend the evening licking the nuts off a large Neapolitan.

SAMANTHA ON THE POLICE

Samantha has been trying some suspects at the Old Bailey. When it comes to criminals there's nothing she finds more satisfying than hardened ones being put away by the Yard.

SAMANTHA ON THE PROPERTY MARKET

Samantha is currently selling her seaside apartment so is dealing with estate agents. She says she's got a man coming round who's keen to inspect her flat out on the beach.

SAMANTHA ON 'I'M SORRY I HAVEN'T A CLUE'

Samantha wasn't with the teams for the first recording. Having just won 'Longest Legs of the Year 1972', she was in great demand for supermarket promotion work, and was busy opening them several times a day.

SAMANTHA ON HORSES

Samantha is off to meet a local racehorse owner. She's a keen horse-woman and he's offered her the chance of a couple of races he'd like her to contest. She says it's a great opportunity as he's prepared to drop his usual jockeys and enter her at Doncaster.

SAMANTHA ON RADIO 2

Samantha is often to be seen sampling beers and whiskies at the Radio 2 party. She says most years she expects to enjoy having a pint and a stiff Johnnie Walker chaser.

SAMANTHA WINE TASTING

Samantha was invited to a tasting by a gentleman wine merchant. He'd brought in a selection of French whites but there wasn't much left by the time Samantha got there. So, although she was disappointed he only had a Semillon, she thought it would be impolite not to taste it anyway.

SAMANTHA ON BEES

Samantha has recently started keeping bees and already has three dozen or so. She has an expert handler who comes round to give her demonstrations. He'll carefully take out her 38 bees and soon has them flying around his head.

SAMANTHA ON THE WEST COUNTRY

Samantha has a businessman friend in Somerset who's recently planted an apple orchard with a view to getting into commercial scrumpy production. Samantha says if his forecasts are correct, he's going to be really big in cider.

SAMANTHA ON THE NHS

Samantha likes to meet with a gentleman friend in an NHS hospital where he's the anaesthetist. He introduces her to some of his patients, and if she's lucky, sometimes even knocks one out in front of her.

SAMANTHA ON THE NAVY

Samantha once had to attend the funeral of an elderly naval gentlemen friend near Tower Bridge. She said she took his ashes aboard HMS 'Belfast', and as his former crew stood proudly to attention, Samantha solemnly tossed them over the side.

SAMANTHA ON DOING GOOD TURNS

When she's not at the scoring desk, Samantha often runs errands for the recording crew, such as nipping out to fetch their sandwiches. Their favourite treat is cheese with home-made chutney, but they never object when she palms them off with relish.

SAMANTHA ON HORTICULTURE

Samantha does a few garden chores for an elderly gentleman who lives nearby. Last weekend she pruned his fruit trees, while he sat in a deckchair and watched her beaver away up the ladder.

SAMANTHA ON THE BBC GRAMOPHONE LIBRARY

Samantha often visits the BBC gramophone library to research the teams' records. It's pitch black down there, so Samantha and the elderly archivist have taken to searching the shelves by candlelight, which can be messy. So while Samantha passes down the discs, the nice man holds the ladder while he cleans the dust and wax off in the dark.

SAMANTHA ON HER ELECTRICAL WIRING

Samantha has a recurring problem with faulty wiring, and yet another electrician is coming round to check her fuses. Samantha says she blows three or four a week in the cupboard under the stairs.

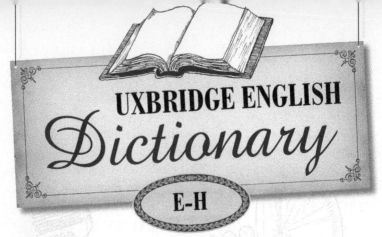

UXBRIDGE ENGLISH
Dictionary

E–H

Fig.4. Eye-glass

Expensive
Formerly thoughtful

Eye-glass
A goblet made by Apple

Eyeliner
A big ship made by Apple

Eyesore
A carpentry tool made by Apple

Earwig
A present for someone who's got everything

Easily
Like an easel

Fajitas
What they use gas for in Newcastle

Farcical
A bike that makes you look stupid

Farting
Something a long way from an Irishman

Flabbergasted
Appalled at how much weight you've put on

Flagrant
Tramp with a whip

Floral
Foreplay on the carpet

Fig.5. Farcical

Fig.6. Gelatine

Gelatine
A device for cutting the heads off jelly babies

Gentile
Where they keep the men's products in a supermarket

Granary
An old folks' home

Grandee
Jack's grandmother

Gringo
Mexican traffic lights

Hamas
What Geordies use to bang nails in

Herbicide
The murder of a Volkswagen Beetle

Hoarding
A prostitute's microwave

Hob goblin
Anthony Worrall Thompson

Hobnob
A cooking accident

Horticulturist
Brian Sewell

Fig.7. Herbicide

Cinema Straplines

Our regular team members are no strangers to the world of movie-making. When Graeme Garden starred in a remake of 'Planet of the Apes', he had to spend eight hours every day in make-up, having big yellow teeth and huge hairy nostrils expertly disguised. And Tim Brooke-Taylor was at Paramount Studios, where he spent days getting his lines word-perfect: 'Who takes milk, and who takes sugar?'

MEMOIRS OF AN INVISIBLE MAN

Women want him for his wit.
The CIA wants him for his body.
All Nick wants is. . .
for people to stop bumping into him

BABE

A little pig goes. . .
well with apple sauce

ALIEN

In space no one can hear you. . .
& Yours

BROKEBACK MOUNTAIN

Love is. . .
a pair of chaps

BRAVEHEART

His passion captivated a woman. His courage inspired a nation. His. . .
accent was all over the place

CAPE FEAR

There is nothing in the dark that isn't there in the light, except. . .
that coffee table that I just banged my shin on

ALIEN 3

The bitch is. . .
still hosting 'The Weakest Link'

THE LONG GOODBYE

Nothing says goodbye like. . .
a wreath

GONE WITH THE WIND

The most magnificent. . .
clear out

CAT PEOPLE

She was one of the dreaded cat people, doomed to slink and prowl and court by night, fearing always that a lover's kiss might. . .
lead to noisy sex on the garage roof

REVENGE OF THE NERDS

They've been laughed at, picked on and put down. But now it's time for. . .
them to form a coalition with the Tories

GREMLINS

Don't get him wet, keep him out of bright light, and never. . .
call him 'Mr' Sugar

THE SAINT

Never reveal your name.
Never turn your back.
Never. . .
drop the soap in the shower

THE POSTMAN ALWAYS RINGS TWICE

If there was an Eleventh
Commandment. . .
it was lost in the post

THE OMEN

Good morning. You are one day
closer to the end of the world.
You have. . .
reached the Samaritans

SCANNERS

10 seconds – the pain begins.
15 seconds – you can't breathe.
20 seconds. . .
switch off 'Quote. . . Unquote'

WEEKEND AT BERNIE'S

Bernie may be dead but he's. . .
still running Formula One racing

OF MICE AND MEN

We have a dream. Someday we'll
have a little house and a. . .
hole in the skirting board

THE LORD OF THE RINGS

One ring to. . .
let us know you've arrived

THE 39 STEPS

Handcuffed to the girl who. . .
has charges that are very reasonable

INVASION OF THE BODY SNATCHERS

Incredible. Invisible. . .
I want my money back

ARACHNOPHOBIA

Eight legs, two fangs and. . .
why did I take this job bikini waxing Susan Boyle?

PRIMAL FEAR

Sooner or later a man who wears
two faces forgets. . .
both forms of photo ID

COMPLETE Cautions

You can't move these days without being confronted by a cautionary label or warning sign. Once there was just the Public Information Film, the most famous being the one telling us to 'wear something white at night'. As a result, Tim Brooke-Taylor goes out with pages from his bookings diary pinned on his coat.

No animals were harmed in the. . .
making of this burger

High visibility vests must be. . .
rather embarrassing

Ear defenders must be worn at all. . .
Colin Sell's recitals

In case of eye contact, flush. . .
bright red and leave urinal

Contents are ribbed for. . .
all we know

If you do not understand or cannot read all directions, cautions and warnings. . .
this is going to be rather lost on you

In the interests of hygiene, please do not exercise dogs in this. . .
font

Will patrons kindly refrain from running, pushing, shouting, ducking, petting and bombing. . .
during the two-minute silence

If rash, irritation, redness or swelling occurs, discontinue. . .
relationship

Never remove food or other items from. . .
the Harvest Festival

To avoid suffocation, keep. . .
breathing out

Caution, remove infant before. . .
cutting cord

Resetting the clock to an earlier time will. . .
transport you to the Isle of Wight

Warning, if drowsiness persists. . .
switch off 'Deal or No Deal'

Keep face and other body parts away from. . .
Silvio Berlusconi

Do not use on kittens or puppies if. . .
anyone can see what you are doing

During sex activity, if you become dizzy or nauseated. . .
call Lady Prescott and ask how she copes with it

Preparation H Haemorrhoid Cream: use with. . .
gay abandon

'X Factor' board game: fun for the. . .
hard of thinking

If swallowed or used in the ear or nose. . .
you're not using the condom properly

Lux laxatives: in case of accidental overdose seek. . .
a cork

Park at your own. . .
house

Sound Charades

PART 1

The teams regularly perform spoken mimes in the game called 'Sound Charades'. This is based on the old TV favourite, 'Give Us a Clue', which still airs on daytime cable TV, attracting a surprisingly large number of the housebound.

FILM: 1 WORD

BARRY	Dougal!
GRAEME	Aha. Hamish. You'll have had your tea.
BARRY	Oh I had a Maid of Honour and a mouthful of Mazzawattee. . .
GRAEME	Well then, let's away for our stroll up the brae.
BARRY	I'm with you, old friend. To the top of the brae!
GRAEME	Good.
BARRY	Doo, doo, doo (humming to himself)
GRAEME	Och, Hamish! Was that you?
BARRY	I'm afraid so. It always seems to strike me going uphill. My kilt's still moving!

GRAEME	So is mine! Jings, man! The grouse are just dropping out of the sky! You wait here till the air clears. I'll away up ahead.
BARRY	Well, goodbye for now.
GRAEME	Goodbye for some time, I think.

(Braveheart)

BOOK AND FILM: 2 WORDS

BARRY	Ah, Dougal!
GRAEME	Ah, Hamish. You'll have had your tea.
BARRY	Well, as a matter of fact. . . Hod on.
GRAEME	I'm hodding, I'm hodding.
BARRY	What's that peeping out of your sporran?
GRAEME	Oh that, that. That's my. . . Ning.
BARRY	You tell your grandchildren about a thing like this. I've never seen a Ning before. Get it out and give us a proper look.
GRAEME	Oh ho. Easier said than done, Hamish.
BARRY	Why's that?
GRAEME	Well you see, your Ning isn't much of a one for company.
BARRY	You mean he's not comfortable with strangers?
GRAEME	Oh no he isn't. And that's why he's called. . .
BARRY	Dot. . . dot. . . dot. . .

(The Shining)

JEREMY	*(Falsetto)* Hey, you!
TIM	You talking to me?
JEREMY	Yeah, you. Mezzo.
TIM	Nobody calls me Mezzo.
JEREMY	What do they call you?
TIM	Shorty.
JEREMY	OK, Shorty. I gotta job for you.
TIM	What kinda job?
JEREMY	Saturday morning. It's a wedding.
TIM	You sure it's a wedding? I don't want no funeral.
JEREMY	Ain't gonna be no funeral.
TIM	What if someone 'sings'?
JEREMY	You're supposed to sing. Like a canary.
TIM	I ain't no fuckin' canary.
JEREMY	Listen. You gotta sing 'Oh for the Wings of a Dove'.
TIM	You're fuckin' with me.
JEREMY	No, I ain't fuckin' with you, you fuck.
TIM	The end. Of our careers.

(The Sopranos)

FILM: 5 WORDS

GRAEME Hamish!

BARRY Dougal. You'll have had your tea. . .

GRAEME Well, do you know I've been taking tea and honey with Mrs Naughtie.

BARRY Jings! Does she produce the honey herself?

GRAEME No no, that's not nature's way. She's got a hive on her allotment.

BARRY Oh, I had one of those once. Couldn't ride my bicycle for a week.

GRAEME Mind you, Hamish, it is the smallest hive I've ever seen. You wouldn't think she'd get a whole swarm in there.

BARRY Oh, have you not heard? She doesn't have a swarm, Dougal, she just has the one.

GRAEME Oh that's right. But that's funny – I haven't seen it around lately.

BARRY No no, it's away on its summer break.

GRAEME Really? Where does it go to?

BARRY Well, hers has a time-share in a holiday hive in Monaco.

GRAEME Monaco? Oh well, that explains everything. Goodbye.

BARRY Goodbye.

(Herbie Goes to Monte Carlo)

10 THINGS YOU NEVER KNEW ABOUT

Colin Sell

1   Following Colin's first professional performance at a Young Farmers' Set-a-Side and Subsidy charity hop near Cirencester, the 'Farmers' Weekly' report of the event seemed very enthusiastic. However, the line: 'Colin Sell's playing was much enhanced when he had a go at singing as well' was in fact a printing error and should have read '. . . when he had a goat singing as well'.

2   Last year Colin was invited to play at a special U2 gig. What fine reunion dances those German submarine crews enjoy.

3   In 1986, Bob Geldof asked Colin to go to Wembley for Band Aid. But when he got there he found the chemist's was shut, so he had to buy them at Boots in Dollis Hill instead.

4   Back in the 1970s, Colin once produced 10cc. But the doctor needed a bigger sample and asked him to try again with the tap running.

5   For three years running, Colin has won the award for 'Best Use of Harmony'. The Royal Society of Hairdressers say he cleverly uses it to keep the fringe out of his eyes, giving total control without ever becoming too greasy.

6   Whenever top professional musicians hear the name 'Colin Sell' they are always keen for news of the 'Old Maestro'. At the moment it's being welded up after failing its MOT again, so Colin's back to using his scooter.

7   It has recently been discovered that
     Colin has perfect pitch. So if your
     garage roof needs re-felting, why not
     give him a call?

8   Colin's piano playing is believed
     by faith healers to hold miraculous
     powers. It once made a blind man deaf.

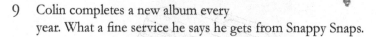

9   Colin completes a new album every
     year. What a fine service he says he gets from Snappy Snaps.

10   There's many a pianist who would give their right arm to play
     like Colin Sell. In fact, losing an arm would be a very good way
     to perfect the technique.

AND 10 THINGS YOU PROBABLY DID

1   Colin's first TV appearance was when he played the mouth
     organ in Black Lace. 'Opportunity Knocks' said it was the worst
     novelty act they'd ever had on the show.

2   Colin has recently been entertaining sailors on a non-stop tour
     of sea areas and inshore waters, and was reviewed briefly in the
     influential 'Shipping Forecast Gazette'. It read: 'Mainly variable,
     becoming poor.'

3   Colin's musical influences are known to be Middle Eastern in
     origin. Mostly Shiite.

4   Colin was once asked to give a talk at the Richard Wagner
     Society after they'd heard he had mastered the full complexity
     of the 'Ring Cycle'. However, after sitting through a three-hour
     dissertation on his new twin-tub washing machine, they realised
     he had actually figured out how to get the rinse cycle to work.

5   During a recent performance, Colin had piles of underwear
    thrown at him. As a result of the disturbance, Wash-O-
    Matic Ltd have banned him for life from busking in all their
    launderettes.

6   When Colin worked with pop sensation Björk, he made frequent
    trips to Iceland, or if they were shut, she used to send him to
    Bejam.

7   Colin's name first came to public notice when he was asked to
    fire a cannon at the end of the '1812'. The investigation report
    by British Transport Police said that if his aim had been better
    he would have destroyed the entire buffet car.

8   Colin has recently decided he'd like to branch into artist
    management and has a dream of handling the Spice Girls. Mrs
    Sell says it's the only thing that gets him up in the morning.

9   Colin says he receives sack-loads of fan mail. Here's an example:
    'Dear Colin, The Vent Axia Deluxe clears all cooking smells in a
    trice.'

10 Colin was once offered the post of the London Philharmonic
    Music Director, but after Colin pointed out that he lives two
    doors along, the postman took it away again.

VERY SLIGHTLY SHORTER
Film Titles

A lot of time and careful thought goes into the titles of books and movies, so obviously the teams take great pleasure in messing them up. The object is to imagine how different these works would have been if just one letter had gone missing from the title. This has become the Holy Bile of title games.

One With the Wind

The Never Ending Tory

Only Angels Have Wigs

Ill Bill

The Pink Panter

Zorba the Geek

They Shoo Horses, Don't They?

My Fair Lay

The Tird Man

The Best Ears of Our Lives

The Way We Wee

O Hello (by William Shakespeare)

The Greatest Sow on Earth

Who Framed Roger Rabbi

Busy Malone

How Green Was My Alley

The Itches of Eastwick

Rear Widow

The Empire Trikes Back

Beef Encounter

Mutiny on the Bunty

The Da Vinci Cod

Lice in Wonderland

Oliver Twit

The Big Seep

Cream

Cream 2

Cream 3

The Prince of Ties

Danes With Wolves

Aging Bull

It's a Wonderful Lie

John Wayne in *True Git*

RECIPES FROM THE
Mornington Crescent Cookbook
FINGER-WIPING FUN IN THE KITCHEN!

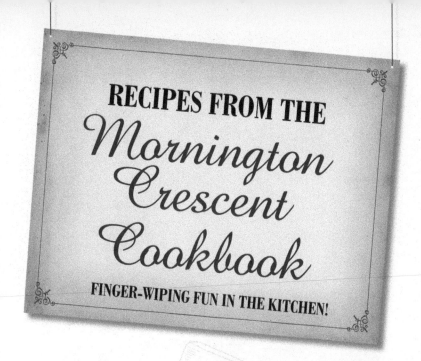

PARSON'S GREENS

A healthy and economical dish to serve when unwelcome guests drop in.

INGREDIENTS

spinach, cabbage, lettuce, peas, beans, kale, green beetroot

water

METHOD

1. Heat 'n' Serve.

EAST HAM

A quick and economical variation on a traditional Becontree favourite.

INGREDIENTS

1 haunch of ham, trussed and passed as fit for consumption

3 litres of oak smoke

METHOD

1. Release the ham from its truss, and – voila!

COQ FOSTERS

Follow any good recipe for Coq au Vin,
but in place of wine use lager

TUFNELL PORK

A popular and economical dish for those unexpected occasions.

INGREDIENTS

4-5 sheets of skag-end of belly pork

37-39 teaspoonsfuls of pork stock or cream

1 medium plum

half a double-sized onion

METHOD

1. Marinade the ingredients in a large earthenware Pot de cochon overnight.
2. Cook in a medium oven [or cook twice in a small oven].
3. Drain off the liquid and thicken with anything to hand.
4. Garnish with scratchings and serve.

BRENT CROSS BUNS

A seasonal and economical addition to any jumble stall.

INGREDIENTS

225g/8lb self-raising salt

pinch of flour

3 tbsps [from the Tbspsina region of Hungary if possible]

half a basin of caster sugar

a generous handful of black pepper

1 large sultana, diced

METHOD

1. Bake in a Delia Bun-Master.
2. Shrink-wrap in polythene.
3. Slip into cardboard box suitably decorated.
4. Seal in Nail-Prufe Cellophane.
5. Stamp best-before date on bottom [of box!].
6. Sell.

SHEPHERD'S BUSH PIE

A traditional and economical regional dish for the ungrateful guest.

INGREDIENTS

1 kilogram [imperial] of mutton, freshly cut from a pre-cooked sheep

6 eating potatoes

1 packet of instant carrot

1 frozen onion

3 parsleys

a cupful of wet breadcrumbs

lemongrass and jalapeños to taste

METHOD

1. Line a baking dish with pastry.
2. Mince the eels and haddock together with the turnip, and form into 'torpedoes'.
3. Spit roast over a barbecue [mark 7].
4. Prepare the custard separately, and serve tepid.

ELEPHANT AND CASSEROLE

A tasty and economical way to use up those menagerie left-overs.

INGREDIENTS

elephant scraps

juice of half a lemon

nutmeg

thyme

1 small turnip

37 other small turnips

many onions

METHOD

1. Simmer ingredients together over a low heat for 2-3 days, stirring occasionally.
2. Serve with celery sticks.

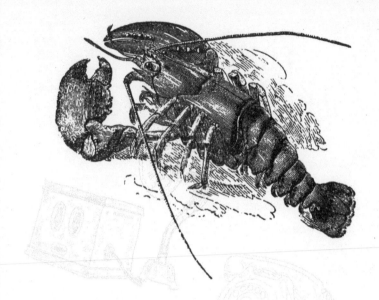

NOTTING HILL GATEAU

A nourishing and economical addition to the tea-table.

INGREDIENTS

8 oz plain flour

8 oz attractive flour

1 knob of sugar

1 tub of healthy-alternative butter substitute

chocolate flavouring E19483754

3 eggs [scotch]

6 anchovy tails

METHOD

1. Beat the ingredients together in a bowl.
2. Pour into a cake-tin or bucket.
3. Brûlé with a Gary-Pro Blo-torch.
4. Steam over a bain-marie, pricking every 35-40 seconds.
5. Turn out when cold.
6. Slice and serve with buttered pickles.

COMPLETE
Biographies

The teams are no strangers to the world of books. After seven years' hard graft, Graeme Garden has just finished his first novel. But then he always was a slow reader. Barry Cryer's biography – 'My Life Was a Joke', was recently published and relates the roller-coaster of success, fame and fortune enjoyed by the many people he's heard of.

KATIE PRICE AND PETER ANDRE
Too Much In. . . *formation*
(Too Much In Love)

LADY GAGA
Behind the. . . *Bike Sheds*
(Behind the Fame)

TIGER WOODS
How I Play. . . *Around*
(How I Play Golf)

C.S. LEWIS
Surprised by. . . *W.H. Auden in the Shower*
(Surprised by Joy)

JACK DEE
Thanks for. . . *Buying This Book*
(Thanks for Nothing)

OZZY OSBOURNE
I Am. . . *Er. . .*
(I Am Ozzy)

CHRIS EVANS
It's Not. . . *Really Ginger*
(It's Not What You Think)

RICHARD BRANSON
Losing My. . . *Credibility*
(Losing My Virginity)

ADOLF HITLER
Mein. . . *All Mine!*
(Mein Kampf)

CHRISTINE HAMILTON
For Better or For. . . *Cash*
(For Better or For Worse)

MICHAEL WINNER
Winner Takes. . . *the Bloody Biscuit*
(Winner Takes All)

MICHAEL JACKSON
The Magic, the Madness, the. . . *Mortuary*
(The Magic, the Madness, the Whole Story)

ROGER MOORE
My Word. . . *Is That the Time?*
(My Word Is My Bond)

JOHN PRESCOTT
Pulling No. . . *Secretaries*
(Pulling No Punches)

JEFFREY ARCHER
In for a. . . *Stretch*
(In for a Penny)

MOTHER TERESA OF CALCUTTA
My Life. . . *as a Pickled Walnut Impersonator*
(My Life for the Poor)

DONALD TRUMP
No Such Thing as. . . *a Bad Hair Day*
(No Such Thing as Over Exposure)

THORA HIRD
Nothing Like. . . *a Good Shag*
(Nothing Like a Dame)

Pensioners' Song Book

The effects of advancing age are all too obvious to our team members. How many of us find ourselves in a room, a bemused look on our face, wondering what on earth we went in there for? The teams find themselves looking at a few hundred at every recording.

Once, Twice, Three Times a Lady. . . comes round to give me a bath

I'm Henery the Eighth I Am. . . No you're not

Knocking on Heaven's Door

It's My Party and I'll Die If I Want To

I'll Be Your Grey-Haired Lover with Liver Pills

Twist and Gout

Wide Eyed and Legless with Hot Chocolate

We're All Going on a Saga Holiday

I'm Putting in my Top Set

'A' You're Adorable
'Eh?' YOU'RE ADORABLE!

Pump Up the Volume

There'll Be Blue Rinse Over the White Hair of Dover

I Can See Clearly Now the Specs Have Come

I Can't Stand Up for Falling Down

Walk-in Bath to Happiness

Zimmertime Blues

These Shoes Were Made in Dorking

Do Ya Think I'm Sixty?

Another One Bites the Crust

Papa's Got a Brand New Bag

I Heard It Through the Deaf Aid

Radio Ga Ga

Don't Go Breaking My Hip

Supercalifragilistic-osteoporosis

Whole Lotta Shakin' Going On

The Incontinental

The Hippy Hippy Replacement

Stairlift to Heaven

Goodness Gracious Great Balls of Wool

Speak Up Little Suzie

Stayin' Alive

Gazetteer

PART 1

ABERDEEN

On Scotland's north-east coast

ABERDEEN is a large fishing port and oil and gas terminal. The name 'Aberdeen' is a Scots Celtic word meaning 'a large fishing port and oil and gas terminal'.

During the Scottish Wars of Independence between 1296 and 1357 Aberdeen was under English rule. In 1340, to underline his authority, King Edward III arrived with his bride, the twelve-year-old Princess Isabel. They were married in Aberdeen Cathedral before a congregation of a hundred barons and just after netball practice. However, the marriage was annulled by the Pope when he discovered the couple were second cousins, and consequently far too distantly related for legal royal marriage.

Having been forced to divorce from Isabel, Edward then married a French countess called 'Isabella', as not only did she bring rich estates in France, but it also made for a relatively painless change to his arm tattoo.

Aberdeen is home to the famous Blairs Museum, where, in 2008, Alex Salmond was formally presented with Mary, Queen of Scots' death warrant by the Archbishop of Canterbury. Salmond accepted the warrant but pointed out the Archbishop had arrived a bit late, as Mary had been executed in 1587.

The museum contains a painting of Queen Mary facing her

accusers, who proclaimed she'd murdered Lord Darnley and planned to assassinate Queen Elizabeth I. It's recorded that Mary found the charges so ludicrous, she nearly laughed her head off.

A popular entertainment venue since 1897 is Aberdeen's 'Tivoli Theatre', being given that name as it's a large room with a stage and rows of seats in it.

The movie actor James Donald was born in Aberdeen. His first role was to play a radio sports reporter following the Scotland national football team's progress through the World Cup. His second was a speaking part.

AYLESBURY

County town of Buckinghamshire

AYLESBURY is often referred to as the 'Acapulco of Buckinghamshire', because it makes people want to throw themselves off a cliff.

In Anglo-Saxon times, Aylesbury became famous as the burial place of Saint Osyth, a nun who was beheaded by Viking marauders. Pilgrims to her shrine believed Osyth picked up her own head and, tucking it under her arm, walked back to her convent, where she fell to the floor. She probably tripped over the doorstep.

In the 1820s, an Aylesbury man became Britain's first forensic scientist. It was Grisham Elliot, who devised a system for the storage and cataloguing of stolen goods, in what we now call 'The British Museum'.

With the arrival of mains gas in the streets of Aylesbury in 1834, the town boomed. In fact, they heard the explosion in Amersham.

In the 1870s, Aylesbury was the home of the first Englishman to visit Lourdes. Reginald Hitchins had never walked, and at the age of forty-seven, the city funded him a rail ticket to Lourdes, where he was pushed into the waters in the wheelchair he would never use again. The event was reported by the 'Bucks Evening Herald' with the headline: 'Aylesbury Man Drowns in France'.

Aylesbury's most famous musician was the composer of opera and choral music Rutland Boughton. In 1927, he was awarded a prestigious Royal School of Music Award. Then, in 1948, Rutland Boughton was surprised to be named Buckinghamshire's 'best kept village'.

The aviation pioneer Geoffrey de Havilland was born in Aylesbury where, in 1908, he decided to build an aeroplane. De Havilland spent two years trying to teach himself to fly, which was what convinced him he needed an aeroplane.

De Havilland went on to found his own military aircraft factory and during the Second World War, he offered the RAF his Mosquito bomber. But they said they were more interested in bombing Germans.

During the Second World War, captured spies were held in Aylesbury Prison. One was Mathilde Carré, a member of the French Resistance who turned double agent. Specialising in sabotage, Carré was code-named 'the Cat', because in the dead of night she liked to have noisy sex behind the dustbins.

Aylesbury is of course most famous for its ducks, which still run wild there, but pensioners were recently threatened with prosecution for feeding them. 'We like to toss them stale crusts and watch them squabble for it,' said a spokesman at their care-home.

CAMBRIDGE

Gateway to the BBC

GENERALLY regarded as the finest university city in the world, Oxford is eighty-five miles away. As a centuries-old seat of learning, it's famously said that 'Cambridge has a fountain of knowledge where students come to drink'. How unusual to have a fountain that spouts half-price snakebite.

Cambridge first came to prominence in AD 40 when the Romans built a road to Peterborough. The granite slab over aggregate construction remains in near-perfect condition after almost 2,000 years, despite the dozen or so times it must have been used.

Despite the fact that they were mainly marshland, the ancient Cambridgeshire fens were first inhabited around 35,000 years ago, the earliest settlers having walked from Europe, which was then still attached to England. Evidence exists of many from France occupying the local bogs, as they were so much nicer than the French ones.

The straight Roman roads of East Anglia were constructed to ease military movements by the famous Seventh Legion, who considered themselves an elite force secure in the knowledge that the roads were built solely for their use. The equivalent today would be BMW drivers.

Very much a cosmopolitan city, Cambridge boasts Britain's oldest Greek restaurant. Serving meals only in the traditional Greek style, you have to book at least twenty-four hours in advance to give the chef time to let your food go cold.

Notable Cambridge alumni include theologian Desiderius Erasmus, the most influential humanist of the Northern Renaissance; Sir Isaac Newton, who defined gravitation and the three laws of motion; Charles Darwin, whose 'Origin of Species' challenged the entire basis of Western religion; and Doctor Graeme Garden, who knocked over a cardboard model of the Post Office Tower with a kitten.

There's always much excitement in the town when the University rowing crew defeat Oxford in the annual Boat Race. In fact it's traditional for the eight victorious oarsmen to have their hands shaken by the mayor, while the mayor's wife bends down to kiss their little cox.

During the war, radar was invented at nearby RAF Wittering, and to celebrate the anniversary of the event, the original machinery was recently restored to re-enact its first use. At 8.30 a.m. on 10 October this year, a team of technicians set the equipment running, while at the same time, a restored Second World War German bomber set off from Hamburg. And, sure enough, at just after 9.15, France surrendered.

CARLISLE

A Cumbrian town

THE name 'Carlisle' is derived from two Scots Gaelic words: 'Car' and 'Lisle'. So there you are.

Mary, Queen of Scots spent several years imprisoned in Carlisle Castle. It's recorded that at her execution, after her head had been severed, Mary's lips continued to move. Legend has it, a courtier placed his ear close to the Queen's mouth and heard: 'Hello, and what do you do?'

The county of Cumbria is of course famous for its Scafell Pike. At 3,208 feet, it must be Britain's biggest fish.

To the south is found the Lake District – one of the few areas of England where you can still see red squirrels. These are under threat from grey squirrels, which have overrun most of England except here and the Isle of Wight. Arriving from America, the grey squirrel has the Latin name *Sciurus carolinensis*. As it will be unfamiliar to any readers on the Isle of Wight, it should be explained that America is a big country over the water.

In the 1920s Carlisle was terrorised by Mad Jack Haskins, the Derwent Axeman. He was finally captured and tried, and when it was judged he was suffering from paranoid schizophrenia, was given two life sentences.

In 2005 Carlisle's city centre suffered severe flooding. But thanks to generous funding from London, the residents of Carlisle have been provided with the means to cope with any recurrence: 75,000 snorkels.

Carlisle has the shortest air link to the Isle of Man, although while the Icelandic volcano was erupting in the spring of 2010, Isle of Man Airport had to be closed. The airport manager said it was bad luck to leave the house while the earth-fire pixie was smoking his magic pipe.

In 1941, Hitler's deputy, Rudolf Hess, was briefly imprisoned here after he parachuted in to attempt to broker a peace deal. Hess died in Spandau in 1987, during a vigorous performance of 'True'.

Kendall is the home of the mint cake originally made famous by Scott of the Antarctic. It was on a visit to Kendall that Scott met the young lady he hoped would become his bride. However, on returning in hope of furthering the relationship, he was disappointed to find a Norwegian had got there first.

The former French President Jacques Chirac spent his schooldays here during World War II. As president, Chirac was accused of abusing his power by giving his friends in Paris jobs which didn't actually exist. These included: driving instructor, charm consultant and sanitary engineer.

CHATHAM

On the historic North Kent coast

CHATHAM'S famous Royal Dockyards were established by Queen Elizabeth I on the advice of Thomas Howard, her privy counsellor – the therapist who cured her fear of toilets.

Chatham dockyards were organised by Admiral Sir John Hawkins, who introduced incentives to build enough ships in time to fight the Spanish Armada. Hawkins was soon giving away a free set of whisky tumblers with every ten galleons.

Chatham played a pivotal role in the Second Anglo-Dutch War. The government naval war advisor, diarist Samuel Pepys, wrote on 8 June 1667, 'The Dutch navy would never dare to launch an attack on Chatham Dockyards.' A piece of advice only brought into question by the Dutch attack on Chatham Dockyards on 9 June 1667.

The Isle of Sheppey, the marshy island that rises no more than 18 inches above sea level, was next to be occupied, but the Dutch left after a few days, suffering from altitude sickness.

This part of Kent was the family home of Henry VIII's second wife, Anne Boleyn. When Henry tired of her, Anne was accused of high treason and tried for adultery by the Lord Chancellor, whose verdict was 'very enjoyable'.

Kent's famous Dover Castle was built by William the Conqueror. Standing on the cliffs facing mainland Europe, it became known as 'the Key to England', because he hid it under a flower pot.

The North Kent coast is comprised largely of salt marshes on the Thames estuary and is devoted to sheep farming. As the sheep there graze mainly on seaweed, the lamb produced from them has a unique flavour: a subtle hint of toilet roll with an undertone of marine-grade fuel oil.

This part of Kent holds the record for the warmest temperature ever recorded in Britain. On 10 August 2003, a figure of 38.9 degrees Centigrade (102 degrees Fahrenheit) was noted in a glass of Chardonnay served in the Gillingham Harvester.

Famous names associated with Chatham include the adventurer Albert Thompson. On one of his trips in 1922, in a single day, Thompson shot dead a dozen elephants, seven tigers, two leopards, a white rhino and over forty chimpanzees. That was the last time he was asked to conduct a school trip to Chessington Zoo.

Kent is these days well known for its vineyards. Thanks to 2012's warm, wet summer, growers of Kentish wine say they have a good bumper crop, but it works just as well on hubcaps.

CHELTENHAM

In the county of Gloucestershire

CHELTENHAM is a beautiful Regency spa town known as the 'Gateway to the Cotswolds'. In much the same way that Gloucester is known as the 'Asda of the Malverns'.

Amongst the early visitors to take the spa waters was George Frederick Handel, who composed the 'Messiah' and invented the doorknob.

Jane Austen was a regular visitor and it's widely believed she based 'Northanger Abbey' on St Peter's, Leckhampton, although this is disputed by the Northangrian Monks of Northanger Abbey in Northangershire.

Another noted visitor was Dr Johnson, who went there in 1780 to promote his range of floor polish.

The Cheltenham Gold Cup is a Grade 1 National Hunt chase, that was first run in 1819 and contested by five-year-olds. These days, they use horses. Originally a flat race, hedges first appeared on the Gold Cup course in 1924. So they sacked the gardener. It's run over a distance of three miles, two and a half furlongs, which for those readers who only understand metric, equates to 3 miles, 2.5 furlongs.

In the 1920s, C. S. Lewis visited Cheltenham where he wrote early drafts of 'The Lion, the Witch and the Wardrobe', the story of how four children went straight through the back of a wardrobe. He probably got it from IKEA.

A noted Cheltenham resident was Dr Edward Wilson, who, along with Laurence Oates, joined Captain Scott as scientific officer on their ill-fated Antarctic expedition. He perished in March 1912, along with Scott and Oates, during their failed attempt to open a porridge factory.

Cheltenham is also famous as home to GCHQ – the government listening station. So remember to say 'Hello' to them while you're in your hotel room.

Nearby is the great country estate of Badminton House, most famous for its horse trials. This four-day equestrian event has been won by notable riders such as Anneli Drummond-Hay, Jane Holderness-Roddam, Celia Ross-Taylor, Lucinda Prior-Palmer, William Fox-Pitt and, on one rare occasion, someone with only one surname. Princess Anne.

Cheltenham was for a while the home of Nigel Seagrove, the electronics engineer who invented DAB radio. He was married in the beautiful Saxon church of St Mary's, before the wedding party moved on to the Park Hotel. Guests reported that while they enjoyed the ceremony, the reception was awful.

– 'If that's a ladder in your stocking,
mind if I climb up it?'
– 'Don't bother, I've already got one arse up there.'

Chat-Up Turn-Downs

This is all about chat-up lines and how to turn them down. Tim has a brilliant one-liner which puts off advances from groupies. Whenever he's approached with the question: 'Aren't you Tim Brooke-Taylor from the Goodies?', he swiftly quips: 'Yes I am.'

Where have you been all my life?
Hiding

How did you get to be so beautiful?
Standing next to ugly people

I have only three months to live.
I'll wait

What sign were you born under?
A no entry sign

I think I could make you very happy.
Great and shut the door behind you

Is this seat empty?
No, your personality's in it

If you were ice cream and I were hot chocolate I'd pour all my love on to you.
How do you fancy crushed nuts?

My name is Justin. Justin credible.
My name is Clare. Clare off

What would you say if I asked you to marry me?
No point, I'm bored enough to be married to you already

Oh my God. I thought I was gay, then I met you.
I thought I was straight, then I met you

Do you have a map because I keep getting lost in your eyes?
You'd be at home in one of them. I've got a stye in it

If I could rearrange the alphabet I'd put U and I together.
That's funny, I'd put F and O together

Was that an earthquake or did you just rock my world?
No, I just farted

You must be in the wrong place; the Miss Universe contest is over there.
And I seem to have stumbled into a sad bastard competition

Well, here I am. What were your other two wishes?
Piss and off

Did the sun come out or did you just smile at me?
No, I just had a stroke

TRAIL OF THE *Lonesome Pun*

PART 2

Later tonight on BBC2 we continue our documentary about life in the Middle East looking at people whose upstairs neighbours are Palestinian militants. That's:

`Homes under the Hamas`

Tonight sees the first episode of our new drama series set in the emergency room of a busy cottage hospital in Devon. At nine o'clock tune into:

`Ooo R`

Tonight Stephen Fry tests the general knowledge of his guests in the popular quiz from Newcastle. That's:

`Y.I.`

Tonight at 9 p.m. sees the return of Hugh Laurie as the brilliant but irascible doctor who has now had his troublesome legs taken off. That's:

`Bungalow`

Channel 4. Nine tonight. A documentary about the amazing case of a man accused of sexually harassing elephants. That's:

`Tickling the Ivories`

A new series tonight on BBC1 about a hateful hat-maker. Yes, it's:

`Scumbag Milliner`

'Panorama' tonight investigates an outbreak of indecent exposure in Cornwall. That's: 'The Perverts of Penzance'

And now, grumpy old men transfer to Radio 4, so stay tuned for:
`Cross Incontinents´

John Sergeant continues his look at the tabloid newspapers this week and discusses painting societies that have been prohibited. That's:
`Sergeant´s Papers: Only Art Clubs Banned´

A heart-warming documentary where the ladies of the parish get rid of all the weeds in the church cemetery, entitled:
`Let´s All Get Them Out for the Vicar´

As part of our music season on BBC4, we continue our round-table music discussion with the woman who sang 'Those Were the Days', that bloke who sang 'In the Summertime' and the man who sang 'Vienna'. That's:
`Mary, Mungo and Midge´

The Channel 4 documentary tonight follows father-of-eight Dave on the day of his vasectomy. That's:
`A Stitch in Time Saves Nine´

After 'The Archers', Mark Lawson presents a new gynaecological series:
`Front Bottom´

Name That List

This connections game was inspired at a BBC cocktail party when Charlotte Green, Peter White, Rabbi Lionel Blue and Craig Brown discovered they had an amazing connection. They were all named after snooker balls. The object here is to identify a connection between the listed items.

Hamster cuddles, grandma's refrigerator, dog's car and baby's bottom.
All unsuccessful perfumes
(paint colours)

Trapdoor, barking, jumping, spitting and dwarf hunting.
A Norfolk pentathlon
(types of spider)

Ruddy, large, painted, Northern, mountain.
I remember her. Big Liz from Glossop
(all types of tree shrew)

Brownie, camel jockey, frog, pancake face, round-eye, Skippy and orange bastard.
Prince Philip addressing the United Nations
(all racial slurs)

Ice cream, rain, miners, seamen and some mothers.
A good night out in Chatham
(all homophones, e.g. I scream, reign, minors, semen and some others)

Chunky, chesty, flaky, musty, mushy, baggy, pungent and rasping.
Vanessa Feltz
(all are tea-drinking terminology)

Melon-headed, rough-toothed, pygmy, northern and common.
Paul Daniels
(all types of dolphin)

Goatee beards, lollipops, beauty contests, Harry Potter, tigers and the 'Encyclopaedia Britannica'.
All are types of bikini line
(all banned in parts of the United States of America)

Lemons, strawberries, oranges, melons.
They're all bra sizes
(none of these fruit ripen after picking)

Nicole Kidman, Ulrika Johnson and Barry Cryer.
All have been centrefolds in 'Exchange and Mart' – and it was a pop-up Barry
(all suffered from eczema)

Big Brown, Vagrant, Foolish Pleasure, Northern Dancer, Exterminator and Macbeth.
How I grade my stools
(all have won the Kentucky Derby)

Manhole, stewardess, ugly, lazy, stupid.
The original names of the Spice Girls
(all have politically correct equivalents)

Mr Chatsworth, Joyous Errand, The General's Daughter, Blind Spot, The Two-Headed Spy and Somewhere in the Night.
These are all Prince Charles's nicknames for his penis
(all are films or TV shows in which Michael Caine played bit parts)

Bats flying lower, daisies closing their petals, cats sitting with their tails to the fire, wolves howling and frogs emerging from the water croaking.
All signs of the proximity of Piers Morgan
(all are believed to be signs of impending rain)

Trousers, bowler hat, an aubergine, your bum, jelly, a love bite and braces.
All things not to forget on your first day at boarding school
(all are items that Americans have different words for, e.g. pants, Derby hat, eggplant, your ass, Jell-o, a hickey and suspenders)

Backwind, baggywrinkle, bottomry, double ender, gusset and spanking.
The names of the Hobbits in the porn version of 'The Lord of the Rings'
(all are nautical terms)

Bad art, antique vibrators, toilets, lawnmowers, genitalia, footwear and presents for Kim Jong-il.
A conveyor belt from North Korea's version of 'The Generation Game'
(all have museums dedicated to them)

A beard, a cactus, an air bed, a guitar, a tortoise, a garden hose and sheep.
Welsh sex toys
(all have been implicated in peoples' deaths)

Mouse-eared, whiskered, nut-coloured, dwarf dog-faced, gloomy tube-nosed, rusty and hairless.
Adrian Chiles
(all are types of bat)

Gay Lad, the Colonel, Lovely Cottage, Ben Nevis, Monty's Pass, Highland Wedding.
Synopsis for my new book
(all won the Grand National)

Choking Hazard, Ribbon, Pain Killer, Pink Squirrel, Heaving Virgin, Buttery Nipples, Screaming Orgasm and My Fair Lady.
Proposed titles for the musical before they settled on 'My Fair Lady'
(all are cocktails)

Pythagoras, Mahatma Gandhi, Albert Einstein, Thomas Edison, William Wordsworth, Leo Tolstoy, the Captain and Tenille.
They all recorded versions of 'Do That to Me One More Time'
(all are or were vegetarians)

Staying in bed, peanut butter, vomiting, hot showers, rubbing lemon into your armpits and chocolate.
A student timetable
(all are hangover cures)

Oddish, Manky Bellspout, Showpoke, Ghastly, Krabby and Gloom.
New colour chart from Farrow and Ball
(all names of Pokémon)

Fishermen's Song Book

This Is Dead and Gutted to the One I Love

Twist and Trout

Skate, Rattle, and Roll

Get Me to the Perch on Time

Flash Bang Wallop What a Pilchard

Tiddler on the Roof

Anchovy in the UK

Kiss Me Skate

We'll Keep a Whelk Home in the Eels' Sides

Salmon Enchanted Evening

Hey Hey We're the Monk Fish

Bream the Impossible Bream

Happy Dace Are Here Again

Prawn Free

Whiting Shade of Pale

Roll Over Bait Hoven (by Shark Berry)

Stickleback Writer

Baby You Can Drive My Carp

Whale Meat Again

This is a round where the teams suggested rejected opening passages of great works from the world of literature. For all the good that did, it might as well have been the World of Leather. . .

'THE ORIGIN OF SPECIES' BY CHARLES DARWIN

Once upon a time there was a stork and gooseberry bush

If we evolved from apes and monkeys, why are there still apes and monkeys? Discuss

In the beginning God created the Heaven and the Earth

Ooo Ooo Ooo

As Gregor Samsa awoke one morning from uneasy dreams he found himself transformed into a giant insect

A great idea came to me this morning as I was swinging through the forest, peeling a banana with my feet

It was L. Ron Hubbard who put me on the right track

'THE DA VINCI CODE' BY DAN BROWN

Let's start from the principle of papal infallibility

'I would like to help with your little scheme,' said the albino monk, 'but these barbed wire underpants are giving me gyp'

Leonardo awoke with a sneeze and realised he had a code

'Oh that's lucky,' said Robert Langdon, 'here's the Holy Grail'

'I believe I might be able to help you to unravel the mystery,' said Jesus Magdalene

What can I add to the acres of shit that have already been written about this subject?

THE BOOK OF 'GENESIS'

You're not going to believe this

And on the second day, God took a sickie

In the beginning there was a cosmological expansion of space, time and matter from a great gravitational singularity, which came as a bit of a surprise to God

My name is Phil Collins. It was me who thought of the name of the band

In the beginning God set off to IKEA for a flat-pack Universe

Well, would you Adam and Eve it?

In the beginning was the word and the word was 'Evolution'

Nobody was more full of
surprises than Mr Lady-boy

'THE MR MEN' BY ROGER HARGREAVES

Mr Big was the envy of all the other Mr Men

'Well, Mr Bump,' said the doctor. 'Congratulations: you're pregnant'

The Mr Men adjusted their telescopic sights and set out for the hit

Mr Politically Incorrect awoke to find himself surrounded by Frogs, Wops, Huns and Dagos

'DAFFODILS' BY WILLIAM WORDSWORTH

I wandered lonely as a cloud
and rained all over Manchester

I wandered lonely as a cloud
while whistling through my
blue lips

I wandered lonely as a cloud
that floats on high o'er vales
and hills, when all at once I
met a crowd who said, `We're
off to the pub, are you up for
it?'

Daffodils are yellow, Byron is
blue, De Quincey's a junkie and
Coleridge is too

I wandered one October
morn. . .

I wandered lonely as a cloud,
got lost and had to phone
mountain rescue on my mobile

'NODDY GOES TO TOYLAND' BY ENID BLYTON

It is a truth universally
acknowledged that a single
man in possession of a blue
hat with a bell on it must be in
want of a wife

Noddy liked the way Dinah Doll
closed her eyes when he laid
her flat on the bed

`Go on, Noddy, give us a burst
of "Cum On Feel the Noize",'
said Mr Wobbly Man

Noddy thought, `Who is that
guy over there who looks like
Prince Charles?'

Noddy had not had an easy
time in prison

Noddy adjusted the telescopic
sight on his Kalashnikov and
said, `This is where you get it,
Big Ears'

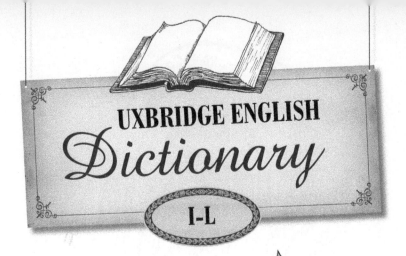

UXBRIDGE ENGLISH

Dictionary

I-L

Fig.8. Infantry

Icelander
To tell lies about Apple

Icicle
A small bike made by Apple

Idiomatic
Foolproof dish washer

Infantry
A sapling

Intercede
Keen gardener

Interlude
A mucky person

Isometric
I so absolutely don't deal in yards, feet and inches

Fig.9. Jukebox

Jacuzzi
French for `I know who did that in the bath'

Jigsaw
How you feel after Irish dancing

Jukebox
What Philip wears for cricket

Kilocycle
A bike with no saddle

Kindle
A state-of-the-art book that burns itself

Fig.10. Logarithm

Lactic
A stopped clock

Ladder
Like a lad, but even more so

Lambada
A sheep with no legs

Lamb shank
Sean Connery's sheep has drowned

Logarithm
Lumberjack on drums

Louche
Where Sean Connery takes his comfort breaks

Fig.11. Lambada

Kindly refrain from hanging your
hats on the Chippendales' exhibit

Unhelpful Travel Advice

PART 1

This is all about deliberately misleading advice for travellers. That's tourists, rather than Romany Travellers. These days we have to be careful not to stereotype Romany Travellers in case they put a curse on us. If they're not too busy roasting hedgehogs over a flaming mattress, of course.

GENERAL TRAVEL ADVICE

Travelling in India? Don't get dehydrated - just order a jug of tap water

After a night out in Bangkok, don't go home without your free ping-pong ball

Australian men like to be greeted with `Good day, Sheila'

Vegetarian steaks in France are called `cheval'

When watching cricket in Pakistan, always ask what the rules are today

In Pamplona, get out in the street and join in the famous catching of the bulls

When packing for Saudi Arabia make sure your wife's driving licence is up to date

At the beach in Rio, every day is 'Twang a Thong Day'

The world over, hotel chambermaids will replace your towels if you throw them in the bath. Do not be put off by their screams

TRAVELLING IN BRITAIN

'Phonebooth' is English for public toilet

In Norfolk, when your host introduces his wife and sister, be sure to compliment her

When in Glasgow, they enjoy you making fun of their local accent

The old market in Bond Street is worth a visit, but don't forget to haggle

In Belfast you'll see lots of murals on walls depicting great heroes from Northern Ireland's recent past. These are interactive street art, so feel free to paint moustaches on them

Our mail is sorted automatically in what we call 'Bottle Banks'

Our prostitutes stand outside offices smoking cigarettes

WHEN VISITING THE BRITISH MUSEUM

On entering the Reading Room of the British Museum, it's traditional for visitors to sing the first verse of their favourite national song. If people can't hear you they'll go: 'Shh!'

The Museum has one of the largest collections of Egyptian Mummies in the world. Please take one

A useful phrase when in the Reading Room for those whose English is no good at all is: `Ere, cock, where's the filthy stuff?'

Any of the attendants will be happy to explain to you how to play Elgin Marbles

Do have a look at the Rosetta Stone. When you try it out with two or three friends, you won't believe just how high it bounces

Demonstrate your support for democracy by adding your signature to the Magna Carta

WHEN VISITING CHRISTIE'S AUCTION HOUSE

Bring your own gavel

It's an old English tradition to tickle the man holding the Ming

It's considered polite to catch the auctioneer's eye and give him a friendly nod or a wink

Visitors are invited to add witty captions to the Leonardo cartoons

When the man shouts out `Going for the first time', you're supposed to shout back `You do and you'll clean it up yourself!'

The best way to appreciate a Fabergé egg is to boil it for six minutes and then crack it open with a spoon

Late Arrivals

PART 1

AT THE RADIO 4 BALL

Will you welcome Mr and Mrs Questions
and their daughter, Annie Questions

All the way from Israel, Mr and Mrs Ook-at-Bedtime
and their grandson, Abe Ook-at-Bedtime

Mr and Mrs Yours
and their son, Euan Yours

Mr and Mrs Ning-Figures
and their acrobatic daughter, Tumbling Liz Ning-Figures

Oh and here's Mr and Mrs Sorry-I-Haven't-a-Clue
and their Israeli son, Haim Sorry-I-Haven't-a-Clue

From Russia, Mr and Mrs Thaweek
and their son, Pikov Thaweek

Mr and Mrs Bennett-When-Will-They-Stop-Messing-About-with-the-Schedule
and their son, Gordon

Mr and Mrs Service
and their athletic son, Daley Service

There's the Hertz family
with their daughters, Kilo and Mega

Here's Mr and Mrs Britain
and their son, Brian F. Britain, their daughter, Ronda Britain Quiz, their illegitimate son, Master Mind, and their Israeli friend, Topol de Form

Mr and Mrs Tin
and their aggressive son,
News 'Bully' Tin

From Wales, Mr and Mrs
Eptions-Terrible
and their son, Rhys

Mr and Mrs Minute
and their son, Chester Minute

Look, there's Ann Ouncer
and Mike Rophone

Mr and Mrs Sends
and their son, Lou Sends

AT THE DRUNKS' BALL

Welcome Mr and Mrs Tasanute
and their son, Piers Tasanute

Oh, there's Mr and Mrs
Notheroneplease
and their son, Oliver
Notheroneplease

Mr and Mrs Tonic
and their daughter, Jean Ann
Tonic

All the way from South America,
Mr and Mrs Over-the-Eight
and their son, Juan Over-the-Eight

Oh dear, there's Duncan
Disorderly
with Wild Bill Hiccup

Those enthusiastic clairvoyants,
Mr and Mrs Dry Sherry
and their medium, Dry Sherry

Camp 'Arry
and his caustic friend, dry
Ginger

All the way from Scotland, Mr
and Mrs Tura-Bitters
and their son, Angus Tura-Bitters

All the way from Sweden, Mr
and Mrs Tortoise-Please
and their son, Lars Tortoise-Please

Mr and Mrs Policello
and their daughter, Val
Policello

And finally
Sir Osis of the Liver

Listeners' Digest

Amongst the many self-help guides available these days are: Jeremy Hardy's 'Window Dressing for Dummies', and Tim Brooke-Taylor's 'Guide to the Correct Use of Vaseline', which won this year's prize for non-friction. While Graeme Garden's book on poltergeist control has been flying off the shelves.

WAITING FOR GODOT

Do you think he will come?
Probably not.

KING LEAR

I'm going to leave it all to the girls.
You must be mad.
Oh yes.

THE SIXTH SENSE

I keep bumping into dead people.
That's because you're dead.
Oh *now* I get it.

LORD OF THE RINGS

Every time I put this ring on I become invisible.
I'd take it back if I was you.

DIE HARD

Look at the state of your vest.
What happened?
If I told you, you wouldn't believe it.

PIRATES OF THE CARIBBEAN

Arrrgh.
Arrrgh.
Ooh argh.
What's going on?
I've got no idea.

BROKEBACK MOUNTAIN

Get off your horse and give me a kiss.

THE APPRENTICE

You're all fired.
Except you.

BRIEF ENCOUNTER

Hello.
Hello.
I've got something in my eye.
Shall I get it out?
Best not, I'm married.
Oh there's my train.
Goodbye.
Goodbye forever.

WAR AND PEACE

Oh, I'm glad that's over.

ROMEO AND JULIET

I love you.
I love you too.
I'm dead.
So am I.
No, just kidding. Oh bugger.

THE MATRIX

What's going on here?
God knows.

THE CHRONICLES OF NARNIA

Isn't it funny what you find at the back of the wardrobe?

QUOTE. . . UNQUOTE

John Julius Norwich, who said this would be a good idea for a programme?
It can only have been you, Nigel.
Correct.

ANY CARRY ON FILM

Ooh er, that's a big one.
You can say that again.
(does so)

TRAIL OF THE
Lonesome Pun

PART 3

At eleven o'clock BBC2's popular boogie woogie pianist returns with a history of the common potato told in song. Don't miss:

'Tater with Jools Holland'

Tonight on BBC4 a new series in which Alan Yentob swans about being a big ponce. That's:

'A Pain in the Arts'

Tonight on 'The One Show', a report on Mick Jagger's failed attempts to win over a famous model, in:

'A Rolling Stone Gathers No Moss'

Tonight BBC2 meets the man who controversially says suicide is preferable to a tombola. That's:

'A Fête Worse than Death'

Six o'clock this evening, Jeffrey Archer, Michael Winner and Piers Morgan join Alastair Campbell for:

'Vile On 4'

David Attenborough visits an animal reserve and asks should we be allowed to own animals? Tonight on BBC2: 'Whose Lion Is It Anyway?'

And tonight at eight, Anthony McPartlin goes solo in a show where he models the latest underwear. That's:
'Ant's in his Pants'

On Sky later this evening, hear how Andy Hamilton hid his sister's medication in:
'Hamilton Had Her Chemicals'

Tonight on Channel 4, we travel to Africa where white farmer Frank Lee tells us why his deer are not watered properly, in:
'Frank Lee: My Deer, I Don't Have a Dam'

Overweight and bisexual? Don't miss:
'Bi and Large'

In a hilarious new game show, Noel Edmonds encourages contestants to throw squares of pink and yellow cake into random holes on the deck of a ship to see who will win prize-money. Join the fun in:
'Batten Down the Hatches'

At nine tonight, tune in to Channel 4 as Trinny and Susannah help women who want to disguise their enormous bottoms, in:
'How Do You Solve a Problem Like My Rear?'

On Five later tonight, the scandal of mass feather tipping at commercial refuse facilities is exposed in:
'Down in the Dumps'

Coming up on BBC2, Jon Culshaw and Jan Ravens lead the team as they impersonate some of the ugliest people in history. That's:
'Dead Mingers'

Tonight we get to peep behind the scenes at the Bank of England to see the skill and financial know-how required to control the world's money markets. That's:
'The National Lottery Live'

Gazetteer

PART 2

CHICHESTER

On the Sussex Riviera

ARCHAEOLOGICAL research has established that this area was the first part of Britain to be occupied by the various subspecies of early man, and there's evidence that Neanderthals mated with humans here. It's called Portsmouth.

At the time of the Roman invasion in AD 43, the area was ruled by King Tincomarus, but he was ousted by his Roman sympathiser brother, Epillus, who was given the title 'Rex' because he liked to drink out of the toilet bowl.

Under the Plantagenet King John, the city came under the control of Richard Hume, the first Bishop of Chichester, who was responsible for collecting the King's taxes. Hume became notorious for his womanising and debauchery, and when he failed to pass taxes on, King John ordered his bishopric be removed.

In 1588, as the Armada suffered heavy storms in the Channel, many Spanish sailors came ashore here. The peaceful and civilised assimilation of their descendants was recently formalised in Chichester Cathedral, where they celebrated by throwing a donkey off the bell tower.

This area's history is closely linked to the sea and visitors may care to visit Chichester's small Naval Museum. Exhibits include a tattered flag flown on HMS 'Victory' at the Battle of Trafalgar. It became riddled with holes from rifle and cannon shot as it fluttered above the heads of sailors on the 'poop' deck, as they called it afterwards.

Just a short ferry ride across the Solent is the Isle of Wight. A charming unspoilt place, it wasn't until ten years ago that the island got its first and only escalator. Installed in a branch of British Home Stores, islanders flocked to try it out, until, after two weeks, the entire population was trapped on the first floor.

CRAWLEY

The economic powerhouse of West Sussex

ALTHOUGH very much a twentieth-century town, Crawley has two Grade I listed buildings. These are the medieval Perpendicular Gothic church of St Margaret in Ifield, and the ASDA superstore on the Pegler Way Estate. Despite being considered by local standards as something of an eyesore, Crawley Heritage made the bold decision to include St Margaret's.

In Tudor times, Sussex was the main source of iron and timber for shipbuilding on the south coast. Henry VIII's best-known warship, the 'Mary Rose', was named after his favourite sister. She famously went down during an engagement with some French sailors in 1545.

The founder of 'Punch' magazine, Mr Mark Lemon, lived in Ifield and died there in 1870. As a mark of respect that week, 'Punch' magazine took all their jokes out for the next 140 years.

The theatrical entrepreneur Charles B. Cochran was born in Crawley. Cochran travelled to the USA, where he spotted the young Harry Houdini and became his manager. It wasn't until he'd achieved massive success that Houdini realised Cochran was taking 95% of his earnings. But on reading his contract, try as he might, Houdini couldn't get out of it.

Nearby Midhurst hosts the British Polo Championships, and has the tallest church spire in Sussex. If you climb to the top, on a clear day you can very nearly see poverty.

The future of Midhurst's Cowdray Park Polo Club was recently thrown into doubt over sponsorship problems with the Veuve Cliquot Champagne House. But the club members are keeping their chins up. At least they would if they had any.

An eminent son of Crawley is the scientist Professor John Nye. As the world's most respected glaciologist, on one of his trips to the Himalayas, Nye is believed by many to have discovered the remains of the Abominable Snowman: two large lumps of coal and a six-foot carrot.

Crawley is the new home of the British Acupuncture Society. They weren't sure where to build their headquarters, and found Crawley by sticking a pin in a map. And very soon after, Reigate got better.

When the society first opened its doors, they ran training programmes for aspiring acupuncturists. During the first lesson, a class was shown how to stick needles into wooden dummies – and down the road, Brighton and Hove Albion all fell over.

GATESHEAD

In the county of Tyne and Wear

DURING the Industrial Revolution, George Stephenson developed the steam engine here. Stephenson actually began his engineering business working in brass, and in 1829, supplied the giant sundial to Manchester Town Hall. The sundial is still in perfect condition, despite being used at least three times.

The renowned nineteenth-century physician Thomas Addison was born in Gateshead. It was Addison who identified Addison's disease, and so began the trend of physicians giving their names to medical conditions. In retirement, Addison turned to charitable work with the fallen women of Newcastle. He suffered long-term illness in 1860, despite specialist treatment from his colleague, Doctor Arthur Clapp. Famous names associated with Tyneside include the Italian revolutionary fighter and nation-builder Giuseppe Garibaldi, who lived here in the 1850s. Garibaldi was honoured by his nation in being voted Italian military hero of the year, from 1862 to 2011.

The scientist Sir Joseph Swan lived at Kells Lane, with his beloved wife and seven children. Swan found fame and celebrity when he developed the first energy-saving light bulb in 1912. Sadly, from then on, he didn't see much of his family. Swan's house was the first in the world to be wired for domestic electric light. Later in life, he became a recluse, leaving the house only once in his last seventeen years – the day the electricity board came to read the meter.

The guitarist and founder member of the Shadows Hank Marvin was born here. In the 1970s Marvin became a Jehovah's Witness and moved to Perth in Western Australia. In case anyone's visiting Perth, Marvin's full address can be found on our website, so you can go round and knock on his door when he's in the bath.

Newcastle's magnificent railway station is served by several operators: East Coast Mainline have services to London and Edinburgh, while Trans Pennine have male staff dressed in frocks.

As the Tyne docks were amongst the last in Britain to decline, they attracted labour from other ports, including Liverpool. When the last quays closed here, the Liverpool dockers took their redundancies and went into small businesses. Through a skylight, usually.

Gateshead's Baltic Gallery hosted the 2011 Turner Prize. Hotly tipped to win the often-controversial competition was an installation consisting of a Take-Away Burger Meal in a large Styrofoam box. You could tell it was good because the fries followed you round the room.

GRASSINGTON

In the North Yorkshire Moors

THE village of Grassington is in Wharfedale, which was once famous for lead mining. It was the quality of Wharfedale lead that made possible the production of powerful car batteries and put the British motor industry where it is today: in a small warehouse near Shanghai.

The other main use of Wharfedale lead was in the manufacture of rifle and machine gun bullets for the army. However, they now use stainless steel, after health and safety regulations decreed that lead bullets are bad for you.

The local Victorian engineer Joseph Bramah invented the Yorkshire beer pump which oxygenates beer as it pours. This is why beer in the north of England has a thick, frothy head which sticks to the side of the glass, while in the south, it's served properly.

The North Yorkshire Moors are very much reliant on tourism. According to their website, when the heather there is in flower, there can be no more amazing sight. Clearly written by someone who never witnessed a squadron of French Air Force jets crashing into an LPG storage depot.

'Barwick Green', the 'Archers' theme tune, was written there in 1924 as part of a suite by the composer Arthur Wood. When the rarely heard complete work was performed recently, everyone agreed how different the tune sounded without the click of an off-switch halfway through the first bar.

Captain James Cook was born at Marton. When he sailed into what we now call Botany Bay, Cook was amazed to see a proliferation of beautiful palms, mango trees, giant lilies and birds of paradise thriving around crystal-clear waters overflowing with crab, lobster and rainbow fish, and was immediately inspired to name it 'H. M. Prison, Australia'.

It is recorded that Cook went through a form of marriage ritual with a young native woman on one of the Pacific islands, which involved her having his name tattooed. Cook was once asked if it was Honolulu, but he replied that it was on her ankle.

The large German POW camp near Linthorpe was remarkable for the first recorded escape attempt on British soil when a tunnel was dug with a soup spoon by a Waffen SS-Gruppen-führer. In the opinion of the British officers there he should have hanged for what he'd done: using a soup spoon before his fish knife.

The North Yorkshire coast boasts the Museum of North Sea Trawling, which was officially opened by the Queen. But the ceremony was spoiled when Her Majesty slipped and fell into the water. She was quickly helped out, but as she's only four foot ten, was thrown back in again.

GUILDFORD

In the county of Surrey

GUILDFORD is found on the ancient Harrow Way. With its crude Stone Age construction and uneven surface, the Harrow Way is claimed to be the oldest road in Britain. That claim is disputed by anyone who's driven recently on the Guildford by-pass.

Part of the A31 near there is known as the 'Hog's Back' because that's what it looks like, in much the same way the A3/M25 interchange resembles a 'Pig's Breakfast'.

Guildford was the scene for the coronation in 978 of Ethelred the Unready, who was crowned wearing a shower cap, and dripping under a bath towel.

Henry II gave Guildford Castle to his son Richard when he married Eleanor of Aquitaine, making him Duke of Savoy, and so gaining control of the cabbage trade.

In 1189, the largest English army was raised at Guildford before King Richard set off on the third Crusade, making the political commitment to sort out the Middle East problem in no longer than eight or nine hundred years.

Companies based in Guildford include Colgate-Palmolive. After the Queen toured their new toothpaste factory, Her Majesty was surprised to find that when she took off her protective cap, staff lined up to squeeze her by the bottom.

Also based here are Dennis Brothers, builders of double-decker buses. Both brothers died in 1939 within days of each other. That is often the way with bus manufacturers. You can wait for ages, then two pass away at the same time. One of their sons took over the business and diversified into building dustcarts. When he died, as a mark of respect, his ashes were scattered along the garden path, across the pavement and down the street.

In September 1881 nearby Godalming became the first town in Britain to be provided with a public electricity supply. And very soon, luxuries such as running hot water and light bulbs are expected to arrive there.

The county of Surrey gave its name to the horse-drawn, four-wheeled, two-seated pleasure carriage with an open spindle seat which is famously celebrated in the musical 'Oklahoma!' with the song called: 'The Horse-drawn, Four-wheeled, Two-seated Pleasure Carriage with an Open Spindle Seat with the Fringe on Top'.

Guildford is the home of Britain's most successful female racing driver, Katherine Legge, who was recently invited to test a Formula One car. Miss Legge was impressed by the kinetic energy recuperation system, seven speed electro-hydraulic semi-automatic gearbox and wing drag reduction controls, but she didn't like the colour.

LEEDS

In West Yorkshire

LEEDS was first established in the sixth century with the name 'Lowides', which in later documents is variously recorded as Lodedas, Ledsti and Ledstantun, before settling on Leeds, after the town clerk was given a pair of reading glasses.

Until it was conquered by the Londis people's leader Edwin, the settlement had been a fiefdom of Athelstan the Long Arm. Athelstan's Britons migrated south, with many finding their way to northern France. Ties with their French cousins are still celebrated here annually with the Leeds International Urinating in the Street Festival.

The eighteenth-century cabinet maker Thomas Chippendale came from the nearby town of Otley. Later, promoting style and construction, Chippendale's lectures on carpentry design were often disrupted by drunken women throwing their knickers at him.

In 1816, the great Leeds to Liverpool canal was completed. Built as a joint venture, Leeds engineers chose the design of the viaducts and tunnels, while a team from Liverpool picked the locks.

With the decline in manufacturing, Leeds has become one of the UK's largest centres for financial services such as mortgages and brokerage, with the number of transactions in 2011 amounting to three.

Leeds' Royal Armouries house fascinating exhibitions of historical conflicts. These include the Siege of Constantinople, which halted the expansion of the Ottoman Empire and put an end to the largest chain of sofa shops in the Middle East.

In the 1920s Leeds was notorious for its slums. Amongst the worst was Quarry Hill, with back-to-back terraces of tiny blackened houses crammed together, permanently swathed in the gloom of smoke and soot issuing from surrounding factories. They may have suffered grinding poverty in appalling conditions but that community shared something money doesn't buy: rickets.

Leeds is world famous for its piano competition. The last event was won by Sofya Gulyak of Russia, who actually got two pianos, as it was a roll-over week.

Leeds is the hometown of many well-loved wits and raconteurs: Alan Bennett, Peter O'Toole and Barry Cryer – to name but two.

The leading light of the Young British Art movement, Damien Hirst, grew up in Leeds. At infant school, he drew his first crayon picture of a cat, which looked more like a football with knitting needles sticking out of each side. Sadly, Hirst never lived up to that early promise.

Cheesemakers' Film Club

Cambozola: East of Java

The Edam Busters

The Rock 4

The Curd Man

This Happy Brie

Wensleydale Well?

Caerphilly Does It

Three Men and a Babybel

The Mousetrap

The Whole 9 Yargs

Dustin Hoffman in Toastie

East of Edam

The Danish Blue Lagoon

Rind and Rind the Mulberry Bush

Dairylea We Roll Along

Cheddar Gabler

La Dolcelatte Vita

The Cheshire of the Sierra Madre

The Hunt for Red Leicester

'Cheeses of Nazareth'

I Married a Munster

Water Biscuit Down

Brie Willy

The Gouda, the Brie and the Ugly

The Grater Escape

Far From the Madding Curd

David Lynch's Blue Vinnie

Cheese Straw Dogs

The Guns of Mascarpone

Fromage to Eternity

Philadelphia

Bring Me the Cheddar, Alfredo Garcia

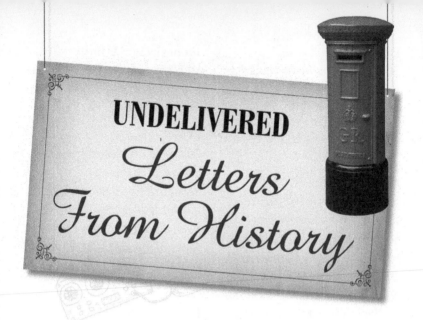

UNDELIVERED
Letters
From History

With the advent of email, letter writing has largely gone out of fashion, to the extent that, before long, the good old postage stamp will be completely redundant. There'll be no more commemorative issues, such as those depicting breeds of British dogs, each stamp coming with a special instruction to sniff the back before licking it. In this game, the teams imagined what effect certain letters might have had on history, had they not gone missing.

Dear Dr Guillotine,
We shall be pleased to grant a licence for your automated haircutting device just as soon as you've addressed one or two safety issues we've identified. Yours etcetera

Dear Mr Logie Baird,
Yes we can grant you a licence to start your new service but only on the condition you never broadcast any programmes with the word `celebrity' in the title.

Dear Moses,
Just to let you know the jet ski is now in stock.

Dear Joseph and Mary,
Congratulations on the birth of your daughter.

Dear Laszlo Biro,
Thank you for letting us see your ingenious writing device; however, we would discourage you from pressing ahead with its development as we will be devoting all future production to the implement devised by our client Mr Johann Felt-Tip

Dear King Harold,
Good news! Your new spectacles have arrived and are ready for collection. Specsavers, The High Street, Hastings

Dear King Henry VIII,
Of course you can have a divorce. After fifteen centuries of non-stop corruption, murder and fornication here at the Vatican, it would be pretty rich of me to say no. Good luck with the diet.
Pope Clement VII

From George W. Bush:
Yo Blair,
You got it wrong. I said we're gonna invade Tie Rack.

Dear Sir Francis,
Thank you for your recent enquiry regarding the Plymouth Hoe Bowling Green. Unfortunately the green has been closed due to a terrible invasion by moles. May I recommend our excellent crazy golf course?

Dear Jehovah,
Thank you for your recent communication regarding the Ark. Unfortunately recent government legislation regarding the humane transportation of live animals has made it impossible for me to include two of every species. However, I should be able to manage one of each at a push.
All the best, Noah

Dear Herr Hitler,
Sorry for taking a while to get back to you. We think your paintings are extremely promising. Do hope you haven't embarked on another career.

Dear Moses,
I'm writing to seek compensation for the damage done by your unruly Children of Israel. Last Saturday night they caused a great nuisance marching around the town about seven times playing trumpets and I don't know what. To cap it all they did severe damage to our ice-cream parlour.
Yours truly,
Walls of Jericho

To Michelangelo,
His Holiness wants the ceiling plain magnolia emulsion.

Dear Joan of Arc,
Good news! They've imposed a smoking ban.

Dear Arch Druid of Wiltshire,
You are hereby advised that planning permission has been denied for the erection of a large henge of stone. We note that although you will provide adequate chariot parking for visitors, the attraction's proximity to the A344 and A303 junction is likely to cause severe traffic congestion.
Yours, Wiltshire Council

Dear Cleopatra,
Please find enclosed the wasp as requested. Ptolemy's Pets, Cairo

Dear Samson,
This summer the fashion is for hair to be shoulder-length.
Toni & Guy

Dear Mr Columbus,
Thank you for your enquiry re. discovering the New World. Unfortunately we are unable to sponsor your journey on this occasion, due to concerns that you might fall over the edge. We will of course keep your letter on file.
Kind regards, Queen Isabella of Spain

To our Imperial Leader,
Hail Almighty Caesar!
He's behind you!

Dear Leonardo da Vinci,
Scrub the sitting – I've got to go to the dentist.
Yours, Mona Lisa

Dear George Stephenson,
Your application to patent a huge mobile teasmaid has been approved.

Radio Times

The original listings magazine has been around since the second century BC, published in Greece by the philosopher 'Theradiotemes'. It wasn't until the twentieth century that Marconi devised wireless to promote his famous pasta dish and Logie Baird constructed a television set with the help of his little friend Boo Boo.

ANCIENT GREEK RADIO TIMES

The Hammer House of Horace

Theseus Your Life

Only Fools and Wooden Horses

Menelaus Behaving Badly

Oedipus Blind Date, hosted by Scylla and Charybdis

Homer and Away

Hector's House

Tonight's movie – Troy Story (shown at Priam Time)

They Think It's All Ovid

A Question of Sparta

Monty Parthenon starring John Cleese, Androcles and Pericles

FARMERS' RADIO TIMES

Top of the Crops

GMTV

Are Ewes Being Served?

Changing Rams

Smack the Pony

Hens Behaving Badly

I'm Sorry I Haven't a Moo

Rumpole of the Barley

Barn with the Wind

Hello Dolly, the Sheep

Tonight's big movie: The Sheep That Died of Shame

To the Manure Born

Racing from Cowes

Fodder Ted

Sheep Dipping Forecast

Rake Your Pick

The Frost Report

The Moral Maize

The Pasture Show

Goat . . . Ungoat

The Archers

Mrs Dale's Dairy

A Book at Milking Time – Bridget Jones' Dairy

Shepherd's Pie in the Sky

Cowpat Rescue

Have I Got Ewes for Ewe

Mulch of the Day

That Was the Wheat That Was

BeastEnders

Only Foals and Horses

The FA Crop Final

FRENCH RADIO TIMES

London's Burning (Hooray!)

Le Penn Behaving Badly

Bananas in Négligées

Hello Hello

Buffet the Vampire Slayer

Merde She Wrote

Quasimodo in Dead Ringers

The Left Bank Show

It'll Be Orleans on the Night

I'm Sorry I Haven't a Cluseau

Who Wants to Be a Legionnaire?

Look Bank in Angre

Live From Paris – Gare Du Nord's Question Time

Only Boules and Hors d'Oeuvres

Two Mules for Sister Surat

Dad's Amis with Clive Verdun

Un Deux Milk Wood

Le Havre Got News For You

Louis XIV's Weird Weekends

Changing Rheims

Through the Quiche Hole

Are You Being Sèvres?

Rambeau

Toulouse Ends

Ready Steady Gaugin

Match of the Degas

Sartre Day Live

Richard and Jeudi

Top Guerre

HISTORICAL RADIO TIMES

Bayeux Watch

Just William – the Conqueror

Half Blind Date

Unfortunately a Day in the Life of Ethelred had to be cancelled as it's still not ready

Watch Out the Venerable Bede's About

Breaking Vlad

Malcolm in the Middle Ages

Plague School

Call My Ruff

37,000 Funerals and No Weddings

Watch Out Cromwell's About

Are You Being Severed?

EastEmbers

BIBLICAL RADIO TIMES

They Think It's All Jehovah

Noah's House Party

Three Wise Men Behaving Badly

Have I Got Jews For You

Challenge Ananias

The Best of Esther

Middle Eastenders

The Exodus Files

Pontius – that was just a pilot

It'll Be Alright on the Night So Long as You Slap Blood All Over Your Front Door

The Samsons

I Love Lucifer

Candid Camel

To the Manna Born

Novel Openings

It's often said that if you had an infinite number of monkeys typing, they'd eventually write the complete works of Shakespeare. Thanks to the internet, we now know that isn't true. In this game, the teams were asked to complete the first parts of some famous openings to a range of books, novels and autobiographies.

REBECCA

'Last night I dreamt I went to. . .'
the shops with no knickers on

THE CALL OF THE WILD

'Buck did not read the newspapers, or he would have known that. . .'
the 'Guardian' had misspelt his name

THE GO-BETWEEN

'The past is a foreign country. . .'
'Let's bomb it,' said Mr Bush

THE MIRROR CRACK'D FROM SIDE TO SIDE

'Miss Jane Marple was sitting by her. . .'
mirror with a hammer

LORD OF THE RINGS

'When Mr Bilbo Baggins of Bag End announced that he would shortly be celebrating his eleventy-first birthday with a party of special magnificence, there was. . .'
a bit of a panic to find eleventy-one candles

POLO BY JILLY COOPER

'Queen Augusta's Boarding School for Girls has a splendid academic reputation, but on a sweltering afternoon in June one of its pupils was. . .'
taking a shower when a large man with a big moustache came to fix the boiler

THE LION, THE WITCH AND THE WARDROBE

'Once there were four children whose names were Peter, Susan, Edmund and. . .'
Pestilence

GOLDFINGER

'James Bond, with two double bourbons inside him, sat back in the final departure lounge of Miami Airport and. . .'
silently let one go

ONE HUNDRED YEARS OF SOLITUDE

'Many years later as he faced the firing squad, Colonel Aureliano Buendia was to remember that distant afternoon when his father took him to. . .'
stand in front of the firing squad and told him to wait for many years

TROWEL AND ERROR BY ALAN TITCHMARSH

'My small fingers traced the outline of the round smooth. . .'
contour that could only be Charlie's

PORTRAIT OF THE ARTIST AS A YOUNG MAN

'Once upon a time and a very good time it was there was a moocow coming down along the road and this moocow that was coming down along the road. . .'
walked into a bar and said, 'I'll have a pint of Guinness', and the barman said, 'There are udders before you'

Curry House Song Book

My Pappadom Told Me

Balti Dancing

Do the Funky Chicken Tikka Masala

Let's Face the Music and Dansak

Korma Chameleon

Blowing in the Wind

Ring of Fire

Poppadom, Poppadom, Poppadom, Dom, Dom

Tie Me Vindaloo Down, Sport

The Curry with the Fringe on Top

I Don't Need Onion Bhaji, I Just Need Some Bhaji To Love

Move Over Dahl

You Put Your Chutney In, Your Chutney Out

Go Man-Go Chutney

Girlfriend in a Korma

Green Pepper Back Writer

Tan Door Re Mi

Rock Around the Flock Wallpaper

Chapati's Over

If You Knew Delhi Like I Know Delhi

Pappadom Preach

Biriani Get Your Gun

Balti for Two

Flash Bang Wallop What a Tikka

Knocking on Heaven's Tandoori

Hello Delhi

The Sari with the Fringe on Top

Mulligatawny of Kintyre

Cumin to the Garden, Maud

Vindaloo Sunset

How Much Is That Doggy in the Vindaloo?

Hey There Bhaji Girl

Prawn Free

Mumbai Bye Love

Theme tune for Some Like It Hot

Pilau Talk

Anything by the Bombay City Rollers

Stand By Your Nan

Take-Away in a Manger

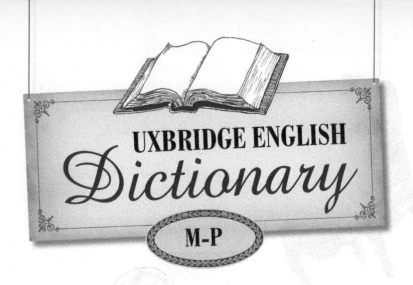

UXBRIDGE ENGLISH
Dictionary

M-P

Macaroon
To leave a Scotsman on a desert island

Magenta
Here comes the Queen

Fig.12. Macaroon

Mishmash
What Sean Connery will do if he doesn't get to church on Sunday

Missile
Where they keep the feminine products in a supermarket

Module
Christmas with the Who

Monkey
Rather like a monk

Nanotechnology
The wife of Grandad O'Technology

Netherland
To fall on your arse

Norway
A surprised Geordie

Ovaltine
A fat adolescent

Oxymoron
Eight members of the BNP

Pantomime
Underwear for the hard of hearing

Passport
Father's race

Pastiche
What Sean Connery eats in Cornwall

Pastoral
Too old for foreplay

Pear tree
What posh poets like to write

Fig.13. Phlegmatic

Perversion
The cat's side of the story

Phlegmatic
Battery-powered handkerchief

Pillage
A pharmaceutically dependent village

Pomegranate
Australian for a Englishman made of stone

Pretext
Letters and phone calls

Psychedelia
Mental cook

Puppetry
Dogs' toilet

Push
What Sean Connery calls his cat

Fig.14. Puppetry

Swankers

The teams don't have much to boast about, though Barry once had a surprise number one in Finland, but then the cold weather often does that to him.

PHONES

TOM   I've got a new mobile phone – it has moving pictures.

DICK   Really? Mine gets the smell.

HARRY   Well I've got hands free, where you don't have to have hands at all.

TOM   Mine's handy – you dial and it actually brings the person to you.

DICK   I've got one that sends them away.

HARRY   Yes, I've got two of those.

TOM   I've got a phone that actually plugs into my house.

GAME, SET AND MATCH

HOLIDAYS

TOM   We've just got back from holiday – Antarctica.

DICK   Yes, it's wonderful. From the Moon.

HARRY   We found the Moon overrun with tourists. Mars, that's us.

TOM   Mmm, Mars is all right I suppose, but not much atmosphere. We went back in time.

DICK   Went back in time?

TOM   Yes. To Belgium.

GAME, SET AND MATCH

CHILDREN

TOM   Children grow up so fast these days, don't they? My three-year-old's got a degree.

DICK   Only one degree?

HARRY   My three-year-old is my two-year-old's tutor.

TOM   I've just had my sperm frozen – of course I had to buy the special trousers.

DICK   Yes, I've just had that – it was my three-year-old who did it actually.

HARRY   Your three-year-old is actually mine.

TOM   Yes, your wife told me that.

DICK   I'm actually in cryogenic suspension. I died 400 years ago.

HARRY   Hence the Belgian accent.

GAME, SET AND MATCH

BARBECUE

TOM   We've got friends coming round for a barbecue – just the Man U team and their wives and girlfriends.

DICK   We've got some nice people coming to ours.

HARRY   We've got Man City doing the catering for ours.

TOM   We've got Posh and Becks over – we're giving them some counselling at the moment.

DICK   We've got Liverpool over to eat the catering.

HARRY   Oh, where's the catering gone?

TOM   What are those sandwiches doing on bricks?

GAME, SET AND MATCH

RECYCLING

TOM   We've decided to save the planet for our grandchildren. We're recycling everything.

DICK   Yes, we're recycling. We're actually recycling our grandchildren. We're giving them to someone who really needs them.

HARRY Why did it have to be us? The gesture was appreciated but we've had to move to a bigger yurt.

TOM   Oh, are you still living in a yurt? I had one of those but I moved out. With the wood stove it's not very carbon neutral. I believe passionately in being carbon neutral for the future, so I have all my farts offset. Every time I trump a tree is planted on my behalf in Borneo.

DICK   In Borneo? Oh dear. Whenever our dog farts I reforest an entire island in the Indian Ocean. And then we eat the dog.

HARRY We bottle our farts. We run the car on them actually. Trouble is as you drive past people shout out: 'Was that you?'

TOM   We keep our car stationary in a hot place and use it as an oven. You can slow cook pets.

DICK   Yes, we tried that. But now we have a real oven that burns Agas.

HARRY Well, we're not fond of eating even and have ceased to eat anything except ourselves and are gradually recycling ourselves from the feet up.

TOM   Who said that?

GAME, SET AND MATCH

COMPUTERS

TOM   I've just bought a new computer. It's got double memory –
         a huge amount of RAM.

DICK   I bought two – nobody has one.

HARRY   My computer's got such a good memory that I've dispensed
         with my own.

TOM   Are you sure about that?

HARRY   I can't remember – what was I talking about?

TOM   Yes, I've got two or three of those computers. In fact I've
         got so many RAMs that I've had to buy a sheepdog.

DICK   The memory's so good on my computer it can actually
         remember when 'The Goodies' was on television.

GAME, SET AND MATCH

RESTAURANTS

TOM   We went on a fabulous holiday and found this little
         restaurant where they do a little dish – I don't know if
         you've had it but it's absolutely to die for – it's a very small
         chicken that they cook for about a week in moss, and then
         serve up with the local cheese and a single strawberry. It's
         lovely.

DICK   Yes, I think you'll find that in my recipe book. I went
         to a place in the very far north of Scotland where they
         actually produced – and this is hard to believe – eggs from
         a mythical bird and cooked them in a special Scottish way.
         Very good indeed.

HARRY   I actually ate the very dish you're talking about and I
        enjoyed it so much I bought the restaurant.

TOM   Well, we went to this lovely Scottish village that only
        appears every 200 years. We had the most fantastic meal. It
        was baby seals cooked in their own fear. It was absolutely
        delicious.

DICK   We ate in a local Scottish village last night – a little Scottish
        village that Gordon Ramsay had brought down specially –
        and the dish of the day was a single tadpole, roasted and
        served in batter.

HARRY   Good heavens! A whole tadpole? Oh, I couldn't eat a whole
        one!

TOM   That's what I said to Gordon and he obliged.

DICK   I asked for some crudities and Gordon obliged.

HARRY   We were on holiday and we went to this fantastic village –
        lovely people, poor but miserable, and so friendly. And they
        made this meal, and they gave us wine and eight courses,
        and they danced for us and they gave us oral pleasure under
        the table and it came to £4 a head.

TOM   £4? I think you might have been ripped off there.

GAME, SET AND MATCH

TRAIL OF THE *Lonesome Pun*

PART 4

And later today Sir David Attenborough looks at dromedary and bactrian camels from around the Christian world in:
`One Hump or Two, Vicar?`

Tonight at nine o'clock Gordon Ramsay studies his family history in:
`Who the F*** Do You Think You Are?`

ITV Sunday at seven o'clock, a team of celebrities tries unsuccessfully to defuse an unexploded Second World War bomb. That's:
`Blast from the Past`

At eight tonight on Channel 4 a documentary by Mr Dee on the unfortunate effect that baked beans have on some people in:
`Jack and the Beans Talk`

In an exclusive interview, troubled pop icon George Michael explains exactly what led him to misbehave in a public lavatory, that's:
`A Flash in the Pan`

At ten o'clock we trace the England football team's track record in the World Cup since 1966. That's:
`Lost`

Later tonight, Ian Wright investigates the shamefully cruel conditions in which mules and donkeys are kept in parts of the developing world:
'Wright in the Ass Hole'

And tomorrow afternoon, 'Woman's Hour' moves to television and becomes:
'PM TV'

A fly-on-the-wall documentary following a group of police cadets in their bid to earn a pilot's licence – that's:
'Pigs Might Fly'

Tonight on Radio 4, a day in the life of Ken Livingstone:
'Have I Got Newts for You?'

Coming up on BBC3, glamour model Katie Price pays a visit to Bakewell in Derbyshire to discover the secret of their eponymous pastry. That's:
'Britain's Favourite Tart' pays a visit to Derbyshire

Tonight at nine o'clock on BBC1, Ian Hislop and Paul Merton return with:
'Have I Ripped off the News Quiz for You?'

And now on BBC3, Wayne Rooney presents a simple guide to double-entry bookkeeping in:
'Double-entry Bookkeeping, an Idiot's Guide'

Later on Channel 4, leading plastic surgeon Simon Wallace discusses recent advances in breast augmentation following successful grafting procedures involving the skin taken from the lower buttock. That's:
'Arse Over Tit'

Coming up on Radio 4 long-wave, former cricket umpire Dickie Bird starts an in-depth four-part analysis of bowling actions over the past half-century, investigating the decline of the full toss or beamer in English cricket. That's Dickie Bird in:
'Nobody Gives a Toss'

At the end of the week we have a home decorating programme from Newcastle, entitled:
'DIY-Ay Friday'

Later on Radio 4 today, Dale Winton goes to visit the Yorkshire Dales, or does he? That's
'Dale or No Dale'

Later on ITV2, David and Victoria Beckham discuss how their marriage has survived both the good times and the bad – that's:
'Thick and Thin, How We Got Through It'

Mornington Crescent

MORNINGTON CRESCENT

GREAT PLAYERS OF THE GAME

PART 1

BROTHER CHALFONT

(AD 520–560 approx)

LITTLE is known of Chalfont's early years, save that he was noviced and installed at Kirkstall Abbey during the Abbotage of Father Rosaenominus in the early sixth century. It is supposed that, following his departure from the Abbey, he travelled widely as an Itinerant Brother, spreading the Good Word and the Received Rules throughout Southern Britain, living on the charity of the good people who purchased his dusters, dish-mops and oven-gloves. He worked diligently as a Missionary, and most notably converted the people of Dollis Hill to Christianity by impressing them with the number of pictures of the Angel Islington he could engrave on the head of a pin.

The Tractus Monkorium of Brondesbury records that 'Chirpy Challie' Chalfont settled eventually at the Monastery of St Ockwell in the Northwood Hills, where he was appointed Brother Attendant to the Poisons Garden, a post which had unexpectedly fallen vacant. His many hours spent in the Library gained him an encyclopaedic knowledge of the Encyclopaedia, and his surviving illuminated manuscripts demonstrate that he was the first to record and define

the 'True and Onlie Rules of the Great Game'. His miraculous Hermit's Abasement from Snaresbrook to Boston Manor is as perfect a Gridiron Slip today as it was then. Respect for Brother Chalfont's knowledge and authority brought him many admirers, most notably St Giles, who often visited him during the holidays.

His contributions to the Game might have faded into obscurity, had they not been rediscovered in the sixteenth century by Bishop Hugh Latimer. The Bishop became a stout defender of Brother Chalfont's legacy, to the extent that he publicly opposed Henry VIII's Act of Six Articles, which directly contravened Chalfont's Regulae Ruislipii, and the unfortunate Latimer was declared a heretic, and burnt at the stake. A Cathedral was secretly erected to the memory of Chalfont and Latimer, and can still be seen today, having been converted for use as a Tube station in 1923.

MOTHER ANNA OF WIDDICOMBE

The Wise Witch
(AD 15??–16??)

MYSTERY surrounds the early life of Mother Anna of Widdicombe, who was born in the late part of the early second half of the third quarter of the sixteenth century somewhere in the west of England. Legend has it she came from a well-to-do family who were amazed to the point of horror by her precocious antics. At the age of three she is reputed to have mastered the rudiments of Mornington Crescent, which

she played incessantly with an imaginary friend whom she treated as the little brother she never had, much to the upset of the little brother she did have.

Records reveal that in 1567 at the age of perhaps eleven, she was taken to London's famous Harley Street to be examined by a child psychologist and then, when he couldn't help, to a grown-up one. The study of psychological disorders was in its infancy at that time, it being several centuries before Freud would formulate his theories of witty interruptions being at the root of human misery. Her examiner concluded she had been impregnated by the Devil, but when Anna explained she

thought a more likely cause was penis fixation, her family disowned her and she was left to roam the streets of London.

It was then she turned to the professional Mornington Crescent circuit, playing the game for money at fairs on market days alongside the cock-fighting rings, bear-baiting pits and dodgy hooplah stalls. Her first recorded match took place at Stepney in the following spring when she beat a young chicken farmer from Wimbledon, Timothy the Hen Man, who went on to be beaten by every player in England during a short and much over-rated career. Even given the Hen Man's ineptitude, the score was quite remarkable. In the first rubber she attacked with Whitechapel, parried the Hen Man's brave but hopeless riposte of Petts Wood with a cunning sideways slice to Aldwych. The youngster suddenly looked lost, and made a last-ditch attempt to recover with Cockfosters but it was too late. Anna leapt to the air shouting 'Mornington Crescent' and it was all over in under fifteen seconds. In those times, matches were played as

best of three, partly to increase the tension and spectacle for the punters, but mainly because no-one had learnt to count any higher. In the second rubber Timothy was floundering from the start and conceded with three moves.

From that moment on, Anna never looked back and as a result was hit by a turnip cart as she crossed Blackfriars Bridge some months later. This appeared to upset the balance of her mind, just as it did the overloaded turnip cart. Times were hard for single women at the best of times, but especially so for one whose only skill lay in what was regarded as a solely male preserve. She played on for another forty years, and though her game skills never left her, and she lost not a single match in all that time, Mother Anna of Widdicombe's increasingly mad outbursts and rantings put fear into simple minds. She was eventually tried as a witch and sister of Satan. As she was punished by submersion in a small pond her last words were 'Get me off this ducking stool' – or at least that is how they were reported at the time.

NICHOLAS LYMMPE

The Infant Repository
(AD 1649–1656)

DURING Cromwell's Parliament the Game was deemed an offence against the State, punishable by death. This was partly due to the Puritans' stand against any form of fun, but also because the Game contained so many coded references to the crown – King's Cross, Queensway, Royal Oak and so on.

Nicholas Lymmpe showed a remarkable flair for the game (his first word was 'Dagenham') and by all accounts was born with a fully developed and encyclopaedic knowledge of all the moves and rules. Unfortunately he was given to blurting out a sequence at moments when Cromwell's spies might be about, and his family was therefore obliged to keep him in a tin box for the rest of his young life. However, it is thanks to the Infant Repository of all things Morningtonian that the Great Game survived the Parliamentarian suppression. The tin box can be seen in the Metal Box company museum at Aldgate.

Primates' Song Book

Chimp Chiminee Chimp Chiminee Chimp Chimp Cherie

The Blue-Arsed Mountains of Virginia

Baboon Ron Ron

Rhesus Christ Superstar

I Don't Like Monkeys

Stand by your Mandrill

Chitty Chitty Orangutan

I Wanna Hold Your Foot

My Orangutan Won't Come Back

Bar-bar-bar, Bar-bary Ape

Tie a Yellow Gibbon Round the Old Oak Tree

Seventy-six Baboons Led the Big Parade

By the Light of the Silvery Baboon

Monkey Makes the World Go Round

Ape Days a Week

Silverback Writer

Simian Smith and His Amazing Dancing Bear

King Kong Merrily on High

Michael Row Rowan Williams Ashore – he's a Primate

Oo–oo–oo–oo–ooh What a Lovely War!

Daydream Be Lemur

Monkey's Too Tight to Mention

Bush Baby Love

Primate Dancer

Ninety-nine Red Baboons

Macaque the Knife

I Want You Macaque For Good

Ooh Ooh Ooh Wants to Be a Millionaire?

There's a Primate Down the Chimp Shop Swears He's Elvis

Anything by Banana Mouskouri, Gorilla Black, the Arctic Monkeys or U2 featuring Bonobo

DON'T KIDS ASK THE *Silliest Questions?*

The hardest questions are often posed by children. Tim was telling us how some years ago he was watching TV with his four-year-old son when he suddenly asked, 'How do you make people laugh?' So Tim sat down while his son explained. In this game we present the team with a selection of difficult questions from a younger listener.

How are babies made?
Well, a stork flies out of the gooseberry bush and Daddy is so amazed he doesn't notice the milkman nipping in the back door

What is the rudest word in the world?
You must ask Jeremy Hunt the culture secretary

Why do I have stinky feet?
You have stinky feet because we can't afford shoes. But don't worry – you'll soon grow out of those old Camembert boxes

Will my cat go to heaven?
He will if you keep on doing that to him

Why did Father Christmas give my brother an Xbox when he is so naughty?
Because your brother kept quiet about Father Christmas and the au pair

What would happen if I didn't tidy away my toys?
The tidy goblin would come and chop you into little bits and file all those bits alphabetically. Now go to sleep

Are Ant and Dec both real?
One is

How do you catch a squirrel?
Unprotected sex with a tree

What does FIFA stand for?
The Russian National Anthem

Will Madonna come and steal me?
Not if the under-bed monster gets you first. Now go to sleep

What's a Liberal Democrat?
Nobody knows

Why is it rude to pick your nose?
Well, it's not necessarily rude to pick your nose so long as you share

Why can't I watch TV all day?
Because we don't have a TV set in the cellar

Is there a Man in the Moon?
Just down the road from Barry's house

What goes tick tick woof?
A dog marking A-level papers

What is black and white and black and white and black and white?
A penguin dressed as a nun riding a zebra

What does 'gay' mean?
Ask your Auntie Norman

Why did my cat die?
Well, your cat didn't exactly die. It went to live with Jesus, who has a small flat under the compost heap

Why does Daddy swear in the car?
*F*** off, I'm driving*

Historical Headlines

Long before the days of computer-based news gathering, messages of great importance were relayed across the distant reaches of the kingdom along a series of huge beacons lit by hilltop villages. Of course, by far the most common message was: 'Help! Our hilltop village is on fire!' In this game the team suggest how today's newspapers might have reported certain historical events.

ADAM AND EVE EXPELLED FROM THE GARDEN OF EDEN

STAR
WOULD YOU ADAM & EVE IT!

EXPRESS
IT'S EVICTION FOR NEIGHBOURS FROM HEAVEN

COMPUTING MONTHLY
BILL GATES TEMPTED BY APPLE

TAILOR & CUTTER
NOW WE'RE IN BUSINESS

THE GUNPOWDER PLOT

DAILY MAIL
GOVERNMENT KNIVES OUT FOR FAWKES

FINANCIAL TIMES
BOOM FAILS TO MATERIALISE

SUN
GUY FAWKES IT UP

EXCHANGE & MART
WILL SWAP EIGHT BARRELS OF GUNPOWDER FOR ONE ASBESTOS SUIT

RICHARD III CROWNED KING AFTER PRINCES MURDERED IN TOWER

DAILY EXPRESS
PRINCE MURDERS – POLICE ARE FOLLOWING A HUNCH

GLOUCESTER ECHO
LOCAL MAN GETS TOP JOB

GUARDIAN
KING ANNOUNCES WINNER OF DISCO TENT

TIMES EDUCATIONAL SUPPLEMENT
CLASS SIZES REDUCED IN ROYAL PRIMARY SCHOOL

SUN
10 THINGS YOU NEVER KNEW ABOUT RICHARD III – 1. HE USES A WOK TO IRON HIS SHIRTS

GUARDIAN
CORRECTIONS & CLARIFICATIONS
`PONCES THROWN IN TOWER`
SHOULD HAVE READ: `PRINCES THROW IN TOWEL`

JULIUS CAESAR'S INVASION OF BRITAIN

DAILY EXPRESS
ROMANS INVADE – NO BRITONS INVOLVED

COLCHESTER ECHO
TESCO SELLS OUT OF PIZZAS

SUN
VENI VIDI GOTCHA!

FINANCIAL TIMES
FT INDEX UP 423 POINTS ON EXPECTATION OF HUGE ROAD BUILDING SCHEME

BRITISH MEDICAL JOURNAL
ROMAN ARMY DOCTORS SET UP VENI VICI VIDI CLINIC

THE DEATH OF SAMSON

THE TIMES
SAMSON OBITUARY: TWO COLUMNS ON PAGE 8

DAILY EXPRESS
BAN SCISSORS CAMPAIGN GROWS

NEW MUSICAL EXPRESS
WHY WHY WHY DELILAH?

THE STAGE
FEARS FOR BRUCE FORSYTH'S STRENGTH

DAILY TELEGRAPH
POLICE CHIEF SAYS HE WAS AN ACCIDENT WAITING TO HAPPEN

GUARDIAN
CORRECTIONS & CLARIFICATIONS DELILAH'S STATEMENT SHOULD HAVE READ: `I LOVE CUTTING MEN'S LOCKS OFF'

NOAH BUILDS THE ARK

NEWS OF THE WORLD
HAM IN SANDWICH WITH MRS JAFFETH

EXPRESS
BIG BOAT TO BE LAUNCHED IN WIMBLEDON FORTNIGHT

STAR
GOOD WEATHER TO CONTINUE, SAYS MICHAEL FISH

WHICH? MAGAZINE
GOFER WOOD COMES OUT TOP IN TESTS

SPORT
MULE IN MIXED MARRIAGE SHOCK

GAY NEWS
ELEPHANTS OUT OF CLOSET DEMAND TO GO IN ONE BY ONE

THREE WISE MEN FOLLOW STAR TO BETHLEHEM

GUARDIAN
CORRECTIONS & CLARIFICATIONS 'WIDE MEN AND WHAT RICH GIFTS' SHOULD HAVE READ: 'WISE MEN AND WHAT RICH GITS'

TELEGRAPH
CAMEL TRAIN ARRIVES EVEN LATER THAN VIRGIN

INDEPENDENT
MIRACLE BABY IN STABLE CONDITION

SUN
YOU WAIT AGES FOR A WISE MAN AND THEN THREE TURN UP AT ONCE

NAPOLEON IS DEFEATED AT WATERLOO

GUARDIAN
CORRECTIONS & CLARIFICATIONS YESTERDAY'S HEADLINE SHOULD HAVE READ: 'NAPOLEON DOESN'T KNOW HIS ARRAS FROM ELBA'

THE TIMES
NEW RAILWAY TERMINUS OPENS – DUKE OF WELLINGTON WINS FIRST PRIZE IN 'CHOOSE A NAME FOR THE STATION AND WIN A METRO' COMPETITION

THE STAGE
WELLINGTON GETS BONA PART

WILDLIFE TODAY
FROG CRUSHED UNDER WELLINGTON

ROBERT THE BRUCE DEFEATS ENGLISH AT BANNOCKBURN

PC WORLD
ROBERT THE BRUCE INSPIRED BY WEB SITE

GUARDIAN
CORRECTIONS & CLARIFICATIONS YESTERDAY'S HEADLINE 'ROBIN THE BRUTE MAKES ENGLISH ARMY SUFFER' SHOULD HAVE READ: 'ROBERT THE BRUCE MAKES ENGLISH ARMY SOUFFLÉ'

FAMILY CIRCLE
IT'S TRUE – THE ENGLISH DO SUFFER FROM PREMATURE EJOCULATION

THE GREAT FIRE OF LONDON

STAR
PHEW WHAT A SCORCHER!

FINANCIAL TIMES
CAPITAL GOES UP

YORKSHIRE EVENING POST
LEEDS MAN SINGED

GUARDIAN
LONDON'S BURPING – POLICE SUSPECT ARSE

INSURANCE WEEKLY
OH BUGGER

LANCET
PLAGUE CURE A SUCCESS

SIR WALTER RALEIGH PRESENTS TOBACCO AND POTATO AT COURT OF ELIZABETH I

SUN
QUEEN SAYS: `GREAT SHAG, WALTER'

OK! MAGAZINE
QUEEN'S POTATO GOES OUT

GUARDIAN
RALEIGH HELPS QUEEN TO CROSS POODLE

LONDON EVENING STANDARD
TUBER STRIKE OFF

Mornington Crescent
THE FIRST CRICKETING BROADCAST

Although several archive recordings of the game exist, the earliest known actual broadcast of Mornington Crescent being played was during cricket coverage. This rare footage features legendary commentators Arthur Pink and Bernard Lyttle at the Oval in 1921.

LYTTLE   Ken. . . Kensal Rise.

PINK   Terribly good. But. . . er. . . ooh, I know, Tooting Broadway.

LYTTLE   Aha! You fall into my clever trap. . . Buckingham Gate!

PINK   Oh my Lord, that's clever. I'm not sure I can parry that. . .

PINK   Oh, look, saved by the sunshine. The rain has stopped, the covers are coming off and the cricket can re-commence.

LYTTLE And yes, at last play will resume in this, the final Test against India.

PINK And with the MCC chasing India's total of 468 declared, England's hopes rest with team captain, Donald Gardiner, and opening bat, Geoffrey Hiscock. As they take up their positions at the crease. . .

PINK . . . I expect you can hear the crowd expressing their appreciation as Gardiner gives Hiscock a friendly wave from the gasworks end.

LYTTLE It was a bold decision of Gardiner to open the batting with Hiscock.

PINK Yes indeed – a lesser man might have saved Hiscock until later.

LYTTLE But what a wonderful find Hiscock has been for Gardiner.

PINK   Yes, a fine fellow who is the life and soul of any party. I met the team at their hotel last evening and found the head waiter playing ping-pong with Hiscock.

LYTTLE As Pootna Shankaranji runs in to bowl his first delivery, and. . . oh my goodness – Hiscock is out!

PINK   The ball glanced off the top edge of the bat, and the wicket keeper caught Hiscock from behind as it flicked over his shoulder.

LYTTLE What can poor Gardiner do now, but watch in horror as the umpire points Hiscock towards the pavilion?

PINK   Well, as Gardiner watches a consolation kiss bestowed on Hiscock by a lady in the pavilion enclosure, there'll be a short delay as the number three gets himself padded up, so where were we in our game of Mornington Crescent, Bernard?

LYTTLE I believe I was going to Turnham Green.

PINK   Oh dear, you could take that two ways. . .

KILLER
First Lines

In this game the teams suggest examples of opening words guaranteed to ruin the rest of the proceedings. Probably the best-known example is: 'Hello. My name's Nicholas Parsons.' Actually that's a little unfair, as those words herald a British record-breaking achievement: the highest number of radio off-switches clicking at the same time. Actually that's also a little unfair, as off-switches clicked not only here in Britain, but right across the globe.

Merchant of Venice
'No thanks, Shylock. I got a loan from the Woolwich'

Waiting for Godot
'Hello, Godot! What are you doing here?'

Bring Me the Head of Alfredo Garcia
'I've brought you the head of Alfredo Garcia'

The English Patient
'What do you mean a waiting list?'

Silence of the Lambs
'Dr Lecter was a vegetarian'

Moby Dick
'Call me Ishmael, or pick up if you're there'

Robin Hood
'Ah, King Richard, you're back already'

Gone with the Wind
'Frankly, my dear, I don't'

Angela's Ashes
'Mam, we got six numbers and the bonus ball!'

Psycho
'What d'you mean my mother – it's me'

Watership Down
'Looks like myxomatosis'

EastEnders
'Prozac, anyone?'

Exodus
'Of course your people can go, Moses'

The Graduate
'That Mrs Robinson's let herself go'

The Famous Five
'Well bugger me!'

The Greatest Story Ever Told
'Heard it'

Black Beauty
'Have you seen how the price of glue has rocketed?'

MONEY-SAVING
Handy Hints

The Handy Hints spot has become a regular favourite, but mistakes have occasionally crept in. For example: whacking with a bolster chisel and mallet is the best way to remove 'tiles', not 'piles'. And when we said that a pair of sugar tongs may be used to pull fur balls from a cat, we should have pointed out that these are in the cat's throat. Here are some credit-crunch-busting money-saving hints.

What's an inexpensive alternative when you can't afford a bath for a dog?
Throw a stick through the carwash

What's a good way to clean the lavatory, unblock the sink, and attract fish?
Get a cleaning lady with worms

What's an effective way to stop a run in your tights?
Tie the feet together

How can you make your bar of soap go further?
Use a catapult

What common yet versatile kitchen item can serve as a foot warmer, a string dispenser and a garden sprinkler, while also helping you save water when you flush the lavatory?
Your cook

How can you keep papers and other household knick-knacks in good order using just a pair of kitchen scissors and some rubber gloves?
Cut the fingers off one glove. Then put it on and write on it: 'Remember to keep papers and other household knick-knacks in good order'

How can you use old paintbrushes to help save on the heating bills in winter?
Soak in methylated spirits, and light

How can a couple of clothes pegs help to eliminate mess when feeding a baby?
Stick one on each nipple

What can be prevented by adding mayonnaise to a child's hair overnight?
His sex life

How might half a dozen lemons and a pocketful of loose change come in useful during a power cut?
Pretend your trousers are a fruit machine. The time will soon pass and it's fun

How can you ensure an almost constant supply of warm water in your house?
Drink 30 pints of lager

My dog suffers from incontinence. What can I do?
You can do what you like and blame the dog

How can I ensure I can find my children on holiday if they get lost?
Dress them up as Taliban

I like fizzy drinks but am worried they rot my teeth. What can I do?
Put them in a separate glass

What's an inexpensive way to remove the odour of vomit from my upholstery?
Fart

Late Arrivals

PART 2

AT THE THE NATURISTS' BALL

Welcome, if you will:

Mr and Mrs Gleebits
and their son, Dan

Mr and Mrs Stichoff
and their son, Lars

Mr and Mrs Anefficiency
and son, Alf

From Paris, M et Mme Habille
and their son, Des

Mr and Mrs Snockers
and their beautiful daughter,
Norma

Mr and Mrs Cheeks
accompanied by daughter
Rosie and son Rudi

Mr and Mrs Vertan
and their daughter, Orla

From Poland, Mr and Mrs
Vestov
and their very keen daughter,
Eva

Mr and Mrs Erless-Parsons
and son, Nick

Mr and Mrs Bigun
and their son, Ivor

Fraulein Emhoff
and her buxom daughter, Gert

Mr and Mrs T'nipples
and their son, Eric

Mr and Mrs Cramsthatintoapair-
ofswimmingtrunksl'llneverknow
and their son, Howie

Mr and Mrs Hynde
and their daughter, Bea

Mr and Mrs Mypudin
and their son, Paul

From Spain, Mr and Mrs Hunglo
and their nephew, Juan

Mr and Mrs Talia
and their daughter, Jenny

Mr and Mrs Jarse
and their son, Hugh

And their neighbours, Mr and
Mrs Janus
*and their son of the same
name*

Mr and Mrs Atthatenormous-
greatpairofknockers
and their son, Luke

From the Vaterland, Herr and
Frau Offmebits
and their son, Hans

Mr and Mrs Tancurlies
and their son, Shaw

Mr and Mrs Tickle
and their daughter, Tess

Mr and Mrs Doesdallas
and their daughter, Debbie

Lord and Lady Bic-Shaver
and their son and heir, Pugh

Mr and Mrs Theotherway
*and their shy daughter with a
lisp, Faith*

Mr and Mrs
Atthathe'sgotahugeone
and their voyeur son, Luke

The Right Honourable Mr
Knott-Snowing
and his lovely daughter, Gladys

Mr and Mrs Willy
*and their embarrassed son,
Everard*

Mr and Mrs Ball
*and their son, who was
involved in an unfortunate
accident with a scythe, Juan*

UNHELPFUL
Travel Advice

PART 2

People in a queue are actually waiting for you to go first

Go to an O'Neill's bar for an authentic taste of old Ireland

Before leaving a public swimming pool, it is considered polite to top it up

Barbara Windsor is a member of the Royal Family

Warning! Pickpockets: Trafalgar Square is now heavily policed. You'd do better in Bond Street

Taxi-driving is a lonely life; encourage drivers to share their opinions

Don't miss Wimbledon Fortnight, but remember to get there early to book the court

It is considered bad form to fall asleep in the theatre, so book a few wake-up calls on your mobile phone

Feeling peckish? On most streets you will find complimentary cats and dogs

Don't miss Trooping the Colour, where you can join in the traditional game of 'Grab the Flag!'

Try a day's raven shooting at the Tower of London

Please do not consult your maps in the middle of the pavement. Zebra crossings are provided for this purpose

American visitors: remember that in Britain you won't be able to fill up your automobile with `gasoline`. We call it `diesel`

Pianist Daniel Barenboim is giving a recital tonight at the Royal Albert Hall, and remember – it's Karaoke Night!

Visit the famous Watford Gap at Watford

Remember the Country Code: Gates are sometimes blown shut by the wind – help the farmers and prop them open

Don't forget to pack your shotguns because there's fine big game hunting to be had at Longleat and Windsor Safari Park

If you see any red and white cones on the motorway, pick them up

If you are staying with a British family, it is considered polite on leaving to pay their council tax

Men – try midnight orienteering on Hampstead Heath

Worthing is fun

Gazetteer

PART 3

LONDON

The glitzy West End

It was in 1703 that the playwright John Vanbrugh decided to build theatres in London's West End and sought funding from fellow members of the famous Kit-Kat Club, but they were having a break, so he had to wait.

Vanbrugh then approached the Royal Westminster Bank with his business plan. Vanbrugh was frequently bankrupt and, as a hopeless, habitual gambler, was a regular inmate of the debtors' prison. So the bank made him chairman.

The borough's most prestigious landmark must be Westminster Abbey. In 2005, newspapers revealed that the Queen made plans for the Duke of Edinburgh to have a state funeral there, but she was advised that royal protocol dictated that she had to wait for him to die first.

The Abbey is found on Parliament Square, the scene of many political protests. In March 2011, when the National Association of Beekeepers marched there, police charged them with rolled-up copies of the 'Woman's Weekly'.

New Bond Street is the home of the world-famous auction house of Sotheby's, who in 2008 hosted a sale of showbiz memorabilia which included the original Sooty puppet. Sadly it failed to sell, as the auctioneer collapsed after constantly hitting himself on the head with his little hammer.

British Telecom have their London offices here in WC1. As part of a Christmas promotion,

BT employed the voice of Tinkerbell for the speaking clock. This followed their earlier experiment with Sleeping Beauty at Directory Enquiries.

The old headquarters of the British Homeopathic Society were in Leicester Square, but they collapsed during restoration work thanks to scaffold poles that were just one millionth of the usual strength.

LONDON

The glitzy borough of Southwark

The borough of Southwark grew in the thirteenth century as the home of the Bishop of Winchester. He founded St Thomas's Hospital in 1215, but closed it again after a few months when St Thomas got better.

At Kennington is the Oval Cricket Ground, so named because it's built in the shape of a cricket ground.

Oval is remarkable as one of just two Tube station names containing only four letters, according to London Underground's official archivist.

The other is written on a piece of paper in the inside pocket of his second best anorak. The other is Bank. Now wake up.

Southwark is served by London Bridge railway station, with lines to the south-east coast. Thanks to unprecedented levels of investment since rail privatisation, these now boast some of the finest bus replacement services in Europe.

Next to London Bridge is 'The Shard', which at just over a thousand feet high is the tallest building in Europe. The architects calculated that from the top apartments it would be possible to see Orpington, so they had the windows bricked up.

Southwark is home to the Imperial War Museum, where there's currently an exhibition of armoured vehicles dating from the First World War. They're mainly crudely converted vintage cars with bits of corrugated iron lashed on with fencing wire. Anyone planning a visit should be quick, as the army need them back in service next week.

Just across the river from Southwark are the world's first deep level underground stations. What is now the District and Circle Line opened in 1890, initially running three trains a day. Obviously, they've cut back a bit since.

Possibly Southwark's best-known part-time resident was the former Labour Home Secretary, Jacqui Smith, who was forced to resign during the parliamentary expenses scandal of 2009. Having claimed the cost of renting an adult video, Mrs Smith's husband destroyed her career single-handed.

Lovers of traditional London food will know Manze's Pie and Mash restaurant which seven years running won the food critics' award for shortest menu.

Southwark is at the end of one of England's most famous thoroughfares: the Old Kent Road. But on the new country-wide edition of Monopoly, the makers are to replace Old Kent Road with a street in Hull with a value of £60, although they don't say what the price will be on the Monopoly board.

NEWCASTLE

In the county of Tyne and Wear

During the Middle Ages, Newcastle became England's centre of the wool trade. Then, when the grazing of sheep declined, mining took over. Deep mine shafts were sunk and men toiled in appalling conditions with picks and shovels, but they couldn't find any sheep, so they picked up lumps of coal instead.

During the early twentieth century, Newcastle became a major shipbuilding centre, but the famous Swan Hunter Shipyards closed with the decline in demand for vessels in which to go swan hunting.

Newcastle is the home of the British Numeracy Society. Dedicated to helping those who struggle with numbers, the society's proud boast is that they're open 24/7, five days a week.

Tesco at Kingston Park is the largest supermarket in the UK. Opened on 28 July 2007, 30,000 shoppers went through their doors on the first day of trading. Tesco say they hope to get them through the check-out any day now.

Cheryl Cole was born in Newcastle. She's the Girls Aloud singer and ex-wife of Chelsea and England footballer Ashley Cole. In 2009, Cole was voted 'World's Sexiest Woman', which was a disappointment, because he was actually going for 'European Footballer of the Year'.

The famous Tyne and Wear Railway System is based on the design of the Paris Metro, so the first section was opened in 1980 by President Giscard d'Estaing. Sadly the President was delayed leaving Paris when his aircraft was affected by a bird strike. Yes, in France even wildlife goes on strike.

North-eastern place names have pretty obvious derivations. When the Romans built Hadrian's Wall, they called the end of the wall 'Wallsend'. When they built a new castle it became known as 'Newcastle'. And when they built the world's first multi-occupancy toilet, they called it 'Middlesbrough'.

To the north of Newcastle is found Town Moor, which provides cattle grazing rights for all Freemen of the City. Historically these rights extend to Newcastle United's St James' Park, but are not actually exercised as a herd of lumbering bovine creatures gently chewing grass might upset the cattle.

Founder member of the rock band the Police, Sting was born in Wallsend. Following massive success, in 1983 the band split acrimoniously. However, in 2007, Sting decided they should re-form, as, although they still had personal differences, from an artistic standpoint, he wanted the money.

Newcastle is home to Britain's second-largest group of Bolivians after London. A hard-working and industrious people, the Bolivians came here to escape the fascist regime and summary police executions back in London.

NOTTINGHAM

Robin Hood country

No history of Nottingham would be complete without reference to Robin Hood. One version of Robin Hood's death is that he was taken ill while out hunting and was carried to the Blue Boar Inn. Weak and fading fast, Robin shot an arrow from his bed and asked that wherever it landed, that should become his grave. Which is why he's buried under an en-suite shower and toilet unit with a Corby trouser press for a headstone.

King John, Robin Hood's enemy, died in 1216, of dysentery, while visiting the Royal Oak Inn. One of their better reviews in that year's Michelin guide.

In October 1330, as the rightful King Edward III approached the age of majority, his supporters staged a coup at Nottingham Castle against the regent, Queen Isabella. Her lover, Roger Mortimer, Earl of March, was swiftly disembowelled and his internal organs displayed on the castle's walls on the morning of Edward's eighteenth birthday.

However, Edward said what he'd really wanted was a racing bike. In the Middle Ages, Nottingham became the first city in England to produce sheet glass for windows. But that was rubbish, so they brought out sheet glass for Windows 7, and that was even worse.

Archbishop Thomas Cranmer lived in Nottingham Castle until 1556, when he was burnt at the stake. Cranmer famously thrust his own hand into the flames. His last words are recorded as: 'Lord, receive my spirit. I see the heavens open and ooh that smarts.' The following day, a freezing cold Sunday morning, Cranmer's ashes were carried to his parish church to be scattered before the congregation, as the path was icy.

Nottingham was home to the first branch of Vision Express, whose original premises were in what used to be the red-light district. One particularly short-sighted customer describes how he went through the wrong door and was shocked to be greeted by a topless hostess. Although he was pleased to be offered the chance to try a second pair at half price.

Nottingham is a vibrant university town, with its own student radio – 'University Radio Nottingham' – where popular local DJ Ray Webb presents the students' daily breakfast show between 2 and 3 p.m.

Construction of Nottingham's Royal Concert Hall was completed in 1982, providing a contemporary 2,499-seat venue. It was originally just slightly larger, but that was before it got into the 'Guinness Book of Records' for hosting the world's shortest-ever game of musical chairs.

Nottingham's twin towns include Ljubljana, the capital of Slovenia. During a visit in 1991, delegates were pinned down by small arms fire. The terrified Slovenians said they wished they'd never gone to Nottingham.

ORPINGTON

Gateway to Sidcup

Orpington is often referred to as 'the Barcelona of south-east London' but only by people who've never been to Barcelona, or south-east London, or Orpington, or have never left their own house.

There is evidence of settlements around Orpington dating back 4,000 years. Stone Age axes and knives have been found in several areas, including Goddington Park, Priory Gardens and on the Ramsden Estate, following police raids on pubs on a Friday night.

Famous for developing his theory of evolution, Charles Darwin lived at nearby Down House. Now in the hands of the National Trust, ownership of the prestigious property was recently claimed by a man calling himself Charles Darwin, purporting to be Darwin's only direct male descendant and so the true heir to the estate. But he looked nothing like him.

Two types of domestic fowl are named after Orpington. The Buff Orpington is a breed of domestic duck whose fine down became prized in the manufacture of duvets. Buff Orpingtons are very easy to keep, but don't let them out of their pen, as you'll never work out how to get them back in again.

The Orpington is a popular breed of chicken named after Orpington. Belonging to the English class of chickens, it was bred to be an excellent layer with good meat quality. In 2011, the Orpington was the most common bird in Britain. In 2012, it was Katie Price.

Nearby Chelsfield is the home of David Griffiths, the computer scientist who developed the encryption system used to make credit card transactions safe. A 'message-to-be-transferred' is enciphered at the encoding terminal as a number 'M' in a predetermined set. That number is then raised to a predetermined value associated with the intended receiver. The remainder, or residue, is computed when the exponentiated number is divided by the product of two predetermined prime numbers, associated with the intended receiver. Failing that, just try to remember your own birthday and your mother's name.

The St Mary Cray Paper Mill Company operate beside the River Cray, where they draw large amounts of water to make their fine quality note paper. In their archive they have the first letter written on it. It reads: 'Dear Sir, I wish to complain about the used condom in my writing paper. P.S. Can you tell your lawyers that was made up for comedic purposes?'

It's difficult to decide what to see first in Orpington, but it's often said that if you only visit the town once, then you certainly won't be alone in that.

SCARBOROUGH

On the North Yorkshire coast

Scarborough was established in AD 966 by the Viking Tustig. Two years later, it was burnt down by his half-brother Lansig. After being rebuilt, it was burnt down by Tustig's uncle, King Harald. Rebuilt again, the town was then burnt down by Tustig's cousin Sanvik and then, sure enough, the entire family was arrested for insurance fraud.

In the opening days of the First World War, nearby Hartlepool was targeted by German naval bombardments. Over 10,000 high explosive shells landed in one night, causing nearly seventeen pounds' worth of damage.

Scarborough's North Bay is home to Peasholm Park – a Japanese-style pleasure park and lake. The park was improved in 2007 with lottery funding, which bought items needed to complete the Japanese theme: a golden pagoda, a model of Mount Fuji and a dead whale.

Peasholm Park's Japanese lake is used to re-enact the Second World War naval battles with model warships. There were also model aircraft, but on 7 December they suddenly flew south and attacked Poole Harbour.

In 2011, Scarborough was voted 'England's Most Visitor-Friendly Town' – bringing dishonour to a previously unblemished Yorkshire record.

Nearby Whitby is famous for its association with Dracula, considered by many to be Yorkshire's finest opening bat.

The crossword compiler and anagram lover George Poulson lived near the coast here. He died crossing a farmer's field, when he was bored by a gull.

Because of its historic sea routes, Scarborough has close ties with Germany and joined in the celebrations of the twentieth anniversary of the fall of the Berlin Wall. Scarborough's mayor was pleased to welcome visitors from the former East Germany – including several balding, overweight, middle-aged men proudly displaying the Olympic medals they won in the 1976 ladies' 100-metres hurdles.

The moors village of Malton holds the largest farmers' market in the North, selling an array of freshly produced 'Keep Out' and 'No Trespassing' signs.

The nearby picturesque village of Thornton-le-Dale boasts a cottage which has appeared on more chocolate boxes than any other. It's the one built in the shape of a Montelimar hazel whirl.

To the north of Scarborough is the town of Redcar. In 2000, Redcar launched a campaign to cut down shoplifting by putting cardboard policemen in their shops. This follows a scheme at Comet, who fill their stores with useless dummies.

Missed Hits

Possibly the most important element in selling a film, book or song is the title. The success of the movie 'The King's Speech' was in no* small part attributable to the purity and simplicity of its title. Here are some less successful film and song titles.

*(Editor's note: No joke here. Speech impediments aren't a subject for comedy. Making fun of stammering is a big, big no-no.)

FILMS

Cyrano de Basingstoke

Indiana Jones and the VAT Returns

Edward Fingerhands

Kiss of the Ciderwoman

WH Smith – The Movie

Seven Dwarves for Seven Samurai

Sleepless in Sheffield

Gonorrhoea with the Wind

Look Back in Ongar

Shallow Gravy

Snickers Man

The Cattle of Britain

The Chronicles of Nan

Bollocks to Private Ryan

Captain Corelli's Manly Grin

Brighton Wok

SONGS

Fifty Ways to Lose Your Liver

I Know Him. Oh Well

Portaloo Sunset

The Tracks of My Tyres

I Bet You Look Good on the Pub Floor

The Newt Has a Thousand Eyes

Sexual Ealing

Everything I Do, I Do It for Money

Killing Me Softly with His Thong

People Will Say We're in Hove

Twenty-four Hours from Tulse Hill

Ah Bidets Are Here Again

Dedicated to My One-Eyed Love

Mild Thing

Ever Fallen in Love with Someone with Whom You Should Not Have Fallen in Love?

I Lit a Fart in San Francisco

I Wanna Hold Your Gland

Meet Me in St Leonards

Bat Out of Hull

Hold On (Your Call Is Important to Us)

COMPLETE *Greetings Cards*

PART 2

HAPPY BIRTHDAY DAUGHTER

Because you are a daughter
Who's lovable and dear. . .
~~Here's wishing that your birthday~~
~~Brings you fun that lasts all year!~~
We're not going to sell you to the
White Slave Trade
For at least another year

90TH BIRTHDAY GREETINGS

Happy birthday to you
and heartfelt congratulations
We really hope you'll have
a joyful celebration. . .
~~So many things have led to this historic day~~
~~And now we celebrate your Ninetieth Birthday.~~
I said: `WE REALLY HOPE YOU HAVE
A JOYFUL CELEBRATION!'

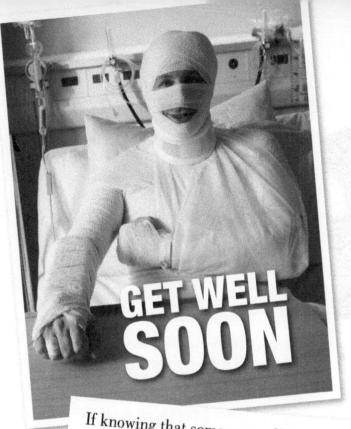

GET WELL SOON

If knowing that someone really cares
Helps healing along its way. . .
~~Then I hope you now feel better~~
~~And keep improving, day by day~~
You're going to be
in hospital
For quite a lengthy stay

A THANK-YOU CARD

You're really very naughty
A right old such and such
I said 'don't give me present'. . .
~~But thank you very much~~
And you took me at my word
You tight-fisted bastard

A WEDDING CARD

As you transform
To Mrs from Miss. . .
~~You'll enter the world~~
~~Of wedded bliss~~
Remember your sister
Who's changing to Mister

AN APOLOGY CARD

'I'm sorry' is just two little words, but they're words I have to say
For the pain that I have caused you, in my terrible thoughtless way. . .
~~Two words I beg from you in return would give me the will to live~~
~~Just two little words are all I ask: those two little words are 'I forgive'~~
Reminder: Your next dental appointment is January 11th

GOOD LUCK IN YOUR
NEW HOME

When the boxes are gone
And you've cleaned up the mess. . .
~~You'll make a home of the house~~
~~That was just an address~~
They won't find that body
Unless you confess

FATHER'S DAY

This special Father's Day wish
That comes with love to you. . .
~~Brings warm and heartfelt thanks~~
~~For all the thoughtful things you do~~
Also comes to let you know
That Grandad's blocked the loo

WEDDING ANNIVERSARY CARD FOR WIFE
OR HUSBAND

Just like a lighthouse on the rocks
Withstanding stormy weather. . .
~~Your love has shone throughout the years~~
~~Stronger now than ever~~
You make a noise like a foghorn
Whenever we get it together

A GET WELL CARD

Thinking thoughts of you today
Because you're feeling blue. . .
~~Wishing good health on its way~~
~~To someone as nice as you!~~
Just don't forget that I am
So much healthier than you

TO A GRANDFATHER

Grandfather, you can always bank on my love
It's both credit and totally interest free. . .
~~Twenty-four seven armchair banking for you~~
~~At the family bank here in my heart with me~~
And as you approach the end of life's journey
Just sign this and grant me Power of Attorney

21ST BIRTHDAY WISHES

Can't find the words to tell you,
Don't quite know what to say. . .
~~The world is so much brighter~~
~~'Cause you're twenty-one today!~~
'Twas I who gave your mother one
Twenty-one years ago today

FOR A NEW BABY

Ten tiny little fingers that always want to play,
That never stop exploring the wonder of today
Ten tiny little fingers that from the very start. . .
~~Will reach out for tomorrow yet always hold your heart~~
Are rifling through your wallet
As your old life falls apart

A PREGNANCY CARD

Deep Within Your Body,
A Tiny Life is Growing. . .
~~Though Inside You Are Nervous,~~
~~Outside You Are GLOWING!~~
Congratulations, darling.
Is that the time? I'm going!

A GET WELL CARD

Who feels good to be alive? Who wants to laugh and sing?
Who wants to leap like salmon? Or jump like lambs in Spring?. . .
~~Who wants to climb a mountain?~~
~~Fly a spaceship to the moon?~~
~~Who feels as good as ever? You will very soon!~~
Not you – you're in traction

EXAM RESULTS CARD

We've known you've worked so very hard
Determined to get through it. . .
~~And now you've made us very proud~~
~~We KNEW that you could do it!~~
You worked all night and then got pissed
Surprise surprise – you blew it!

FROM A DOG NEEDING TO BE PUT TO SLEEP

You will be sad I understand,
But don't let grief then stay your hand,
Today's the day, more than the rest,
Your love for me must stand the test.
Take me to where to my needs they'll tend,
Only, stay with me till the end
And hold me firm and speak to me
Until my eyes no longer see. . .
~~It was a kindness you did for me.~~
~~Although my tail its last has waved,~~
~~From pain and suffering I've been saved~~
I know in time you will agree. . .
I've left a turd behind the settee

ON YOUR DIVORCE

You were several years a-courting
Then marriage took its course. . .
~~It didn't work, so here's wishing you~~
~~A long and happy divorce~~
I just don't understand it
You said he was hung like a horse

A MESSAGE OF SYMPATHY

Sometimes words are inadequate
Our feelings to express. . .
~~When someone whom we hold so dear~~
~~Is in such great distress~~
But just look at it this way
At mealtimes it's one less

WELL DONE IN YOUR
JOB INTERVIEW

Magnificent! Marvellous! Wonderful! Brill!
Talented! Gifted! Consummate skill!
Shrewd, adroit, crafty, clever and porous. . .
~~Outstanding! Fantastic! A1 Excel!~~
~~And that's just the sender – you're great as well!~~
These are all words from Roget's Thesaurus

CONGRATULATIONS
ON YOUR DIVORCE

You were once so very happy
The day you made that vow
But I have noted one thing
You seem much happier now. . .
~~For better or for worse,~~
~~You had the worse of course~~
~~So this is just to wish for you~~
~~A jubilant divorce~~
That she knows you're a tosser
And you know she's a cow

ST PATRICK'S DAY WISHES

We're searching for that clover
The one that brings good luck. . .
~~Four leaves and a leprechaun~~
~~Can never be too much~~
May you be lucky all your life
And never short of a rhyme

A VALENTINE'S DAY CARD

Roses are Red, Violets are Blue. . .
~~It's Valentines Day~~
~~And I love you~~
I'm up for it
How about you?

THANK YOU MESSAGE

This heartfelt Thank You message
Is sent to you today. . .
~~To tell you that your kindness means~~
~~Much more than words can say~~
I haven't put a stamp on it
So you will have to pay

ON THE NEW ARRIVAL

Ten little fingers, two little eyes,
One little nose (button size). . .
~~A wish is fulfilled, a dream has come true. . .~~
~~Congratulations to all of you!~~
Enclosed

A VALENTINE'S DAY CARD

It's that special time again
When Cupid shoots his bow. . .
~~He's aiming at your heart~~
~~He knows I love you so~~
And since you're only four foot six
Let's hope he's aiming low

A MOTHER'S DAY CARD

You were always there as I grew up
You're as lovely as they come
In the lottery of life, I got. . .
~~The all-time greatest Mum~~
A rollover with my Mum

IN DEEPEST
SYMPATHY CARD

Through the pain and loss you feel
You can count on our support. . .
~~We'll be with you, in spirit~~
~~And in mind and heart and thought~~
Best wishes,
The Abacus Jockstrap Company

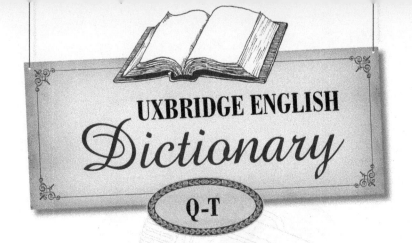

UXBRIDGE ENGLISH
Dictionary

Q-T

Quick
Noise made by a dyslexic duck

Radar
An attack by pirates

Receipt
To sit down again

Realist
A catalogue of bottoms

Rheumatic
A loft conversion

Fig.15. Realist

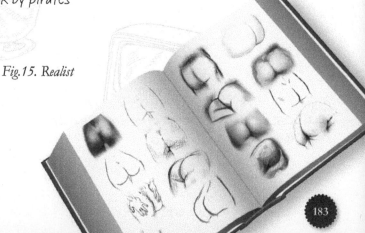

Fig.16. Shuttlecock

Scruple
Cross between a screw top and a ring pull

Singe
What Sean Connery confesses to in church

Shambles
Prosthetic testicles

Shit
What Sean Connery says to his dog

Singapore
Jeremy Hardy

Spoof
Person who only pretends to be gay

Suffragette
Ryanair

Tabby
A big church in Yorkshire

Template
The secretary hasn't turned up

Tenure
How they describe a decade in the West Country

Testicle
A boat maker's first attempt at a coracle

Toll
Where you try to put the ball in on a Yorkshire golf course

Towel rail
Where Yorkshire people keep their owls

Transport
Cross-dressing athletes

Truculent
That lorry you used to rent out

Turmoil
Lubricant for use in school

Fig.17. Toll

Mornington Crescent

GREAT PLAYERS OF THE GAME

PART 2

LORD KNARESBOROUGH

*The Yorkshire Rake
(1740–1815)*

HUGH de Montague Smythe-D'Arrison-Smythe, later Lord Knaresborough, is regarded by many as among the finest amateur Yorkshire players of the modern game. Gambler, explorer, poet, serial adulterer and landscape gardener, Smythe-D'Arrison-Smythe (or 'Flash Hughie' as he was known) was blessed with a mop of auburn curls, eyes of translucent blue and fingers of rich bottle-green.

Even today, rumours of his sexual exploits still abound. Can he really have bedded seven women between Knightsbridge and Piccadilly Circus in a three-stage manoeuvre played to Morton's first stratagem* (and two of them while executing a deft backward triangulation)? Too right he could. What lady, however chaste, could resist a walk with him under his magnificent neo-classical colonnade at Blenheim, past the rainbow display of his parterre at Stowe, or amidst the heady aroma of his tangerinerie at Kew, as he recited Hobbes' second parabola from memory, half cut and gently toying with his luxuriant moustache?

'Chancery Lane –
Holborn – Quex Road
then Mortimer Street
– Tooting – Tooting
Bec – Highgate and
Hampstead West. . .' As
the moves flowed from
his lips like a hypnotic
waltz the sensation of
pure speed must have
been exhilarating, leaving
each one of his conquests
disarmed, entranced and
slightly flushed about the
bosom. There was no getting
away from it; in those elegant,
soil-stained hands, the game
was pure unalloyed sex. 'And',
to quote 'Debrett's', 'boy could
he play!'

At Eton he won the Babbington
Trophy (for Excellence in
the Game) five years in a
row, an achievement made all
the more remarkable by the
fact that he was only at the
school for two terms, due to a
misunderstanding over Matron's
schedule. At nineteen he picked
up the Junior Mornington trophy
after winning in three straight
moves, and by twenty-two he
had defeated Sir Nicholas Busby
himself, official MC player to the
Court of King George III.

Before the age of twenty-five
he'd beaten the French in Calais,
the Spanish in Madrid, and the
Welsh in Tafarn y Bwlch. He
soon came to the notice of
the King himself, and might
well have benefited from the
relationship, had he not insisted
on correcting King George's
dislike of the garden 'ditch';
the King adjudged Smythe-
D'Arrison-Smythe's exclamations
of 'ha-ha!' disrespectful in the
extreme, and he received no
further contact with the Palace.

On inheriting the title of Lord Knaresborough after the death of his uncle (whose admiration for his talented nephew was such that he was only too pleased to disinherit his eldest son and rightful heir in his favour) Smythe-D'Arrison-Smythe wasted no time in introducing the game to the staff and tenants of his Yorkshire estate – with a few variations of his own. To his primitive neighbours he must have seemed like an exotic butterfly, no doubt due to the theatrical moth costume he wore day and night. In fact, so popular was he with the local womenfolk that together they managed to reinstate their new landlord's medieval *droit du seigneur*, despite strong protestations from the Church.

Smythe-D'Arrison-Smythe died outside what is now the entrance to Camden Town Underground station while attempting to demonstrate the Perfect Looped-Shift by performing an illegal U-turn. He was struck by a Hackney Carriage bound for Mornington Crescent under Phelps' second Protocol.

* It became fashionable at the turn of the nineteenth century to physically travel each move in set-piece games such as Morton's first and third stratagems. Less experienced players would hire qualified Hackney Carriage drivers – the experts would drive themselves.

ETHAN JANKS

The Idiot Savant of the Game (17??–1867)

LITTLE is known of the early life of this humble son of the soil, who was to become one of the legendary 'instinctive' innovators of the Game. Born in the late eighteenth century, and believed by many (at least by his parents) to spring from simple farming stock, he began life as a labourer in the Hosiery Department of Tewkesbury's Shoppe. The hours were long, the work was arduous, and he was sustained by nothing more than a daily bowl of thin soup. The first authentic records of his career document his arrest and imprisonment for stealing a bread roll, a pat of butter, a plate and knife, a serviette, and cruet. He was sentenced to life imprisonment.

It was during his long years of confinement in the notorious 'Beachview' prison at Eastbourne that he was introduced to Mornington Crescent, a game eagerly played by the convicts as they sat picking oakum and waiting for their dressing gowns to dry. Janks, uneducated though he was, and unable to tell reading from writing, became remarkably adept at the Game, and his fame spread throughout the local community. He was in great demand at dinner parties, balls, and soirees, both inside and outside the prison, and it was at one of these that he slipped his manacles and made his escape. After many sightings, his progress was eagerly followed by aficionados of the Game, as they saw a pattern beginning to emerge. Uckfield – Crawley – Dorking – Staines – Waterloo – Embankment – Goodge Street. He was arrested at Mornington Crescent.

The sentence of life imprisonment was upgraded to deportation, and he was shipped to Mornington Island in the Gulf of Carpentaria off the northern coast of Queensland. Frail and old, a broken man, Ethan Janks eked out his declining years working as an occasional male model and running a hot-dingo stall. 'Coober Pedy', his Antipodean version of the Game, never took off, and during his brief tenure as Prime Minister of Australia, he died in obscurity.

Costcutters

PART 2

A Fistful of Small Change

Honey I Shrunk the Socks

Lady Chatterley's Loofah

Hannah and Her Blisters

Crouch End Tiger, Hendon Dragon

The Lady Varnishes

Full Menthol Packet

Star Wars – The Empire Cuts Back

Dombey

Those Magnificent Men and Their Washing Machines

Breakfast at Tiffany's Mum's House

Jane Austen's Pride and Precious Little Else

All Quiet on the Front At Weston

Guy and Doll

Night of the Dead Dead

Illegal Immigrant Kane

Lidl House on the Prairie

The Burger King and I

Guess Who's Coming to Pinner?

The Cheap Hunter

Not Bothering to Look For Nemo

It Was Alright on the Night

Jason and the Argos Stores

Nan With the Wind

Unquote

Two Creatures, Great and Small

They Shoot Hamsters, Don't They?

An Evening With Nicholas Parsons

Sabrina the Teenage Reflexologist

Tales of the Inexpensive

Tiny Tanic

Poole Harbour

Downstairs Downstairs

Great Expectorations

Have I Got the Big Issue for You

Three Men in the Boot

How Haverford West Was Won

Bring Me the Hat of Alfredo Garcia

Buffy the Umpire Slayer

A Dance to the Music of Tim

The Pocket Money Programme

To the Semi Born

The Old Curiosity Car Boot Sale

Ready Steady Pot Noodle

The Great Escalope

The Magnificent 7-Up

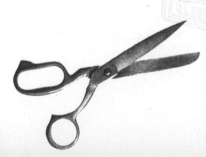

TRAIL OF THE *Lonesome Pun*

PART 5

In the last programme in our pottery season we'll be showing you how to finish the outsides of plates or bowls, in:
`A Guide To Rimming`

Tonight's documentary tells the strange story of Sigmund Freud and his time as a market gardener. Vienna in 1912 saw the father of psychiatry tending his greenhouse at the world-famous café run, surprisingly, by a family of weasels. At nine o'clock tonight you can hear all about:
`Freud Grown Tomatoes at the Weasel's Top Café`

Coming up on Channel 4, elderly relatives get a saucy makeover in:
`Gran Designs`

And now a fascinating documentary about the sensuous love-making skills of Sir Ben Kingsley in:
`Tender Is the Knight`

This week's 'Archive Hour' provides another chance to see gardening legend Percy Thrower reveal his extensive collection of fine bone china, much of which he is able to identify blindfolded. That's:
`Point Percy at the Porcelain`

Next on BBC4, rare footage of a legendary concert at the North Pole's only prison:
'Cash in the Arctic'

Coming up on Channel 4, spiky-haired celebrity chef Gary Rhodes presents his definitive guide to pancake making. That's:
'The Complete Tosser'

At eight o'clock tonight, how Hampton Court's famous attraction was funded by the proceeds of prostitution. Join Michael Buerk for:
'The Immoral Maze'

Later on we see a group of lumberjacks trying to predict how much will fly off a log when they cut it:
'The Chipping Forecast'

At nine o'clock on Channel 4, Gok Wan helps you disguise the bags under your eyes in:
'How to Look Good Knackered'

On Channel 4 tomorrow, a post-apocalyptic makeover programme in which Gok Wan advises on how to deal with the aftermath of an atomic bomb, in:
'How to Look Good Nuked'

'The Complete Tosser'

Later tonight a documentary in which Mr and Mrs Nicholas Parsons talk about their longest night of love. That's:
'Just a Minute'

Unruly garden? It's nothing a few clumps of well-laid turf won't fix, according to Tommy Walsh from 'Ground Force'. That's:
'Sod It All'

Later on Sky1, a programme exploring claims that a small amount of alcohol can have an even more helpful effect than Viagra with:
'Absinthe Makes the Part Grow Longer'

Unseen Prequels

This is a game that looks at the world of cinema. As a professional actor, Graeme Garden is at an obvious advantage. My daughter saw him in a new Blockbuster this summer, and says he was great. She rented three DVDs and he only charged her a fiver. Many famous movies have sequels, but what about prequels? Here the teams suggest movie titles that might have preceded well-known films.

Four Engagements and a Hospital Visit

The Long Way Round the River Kwai

Those Magnificent Men in the Departures Lounge

Schindler's Search for Pen and Paper

I Wish Those Lambs Would Shut Up

Hello, Mr Chips

Nineteen Eighty-Three

Desperately Wondering Where Susan's Got To

What's All That Noise on the Western Front?

Last Tap Dance in Paris

Whistling in the Drizzle

Medical Student Zhivago

Hitchcock's 'The Eggs'

The Eagle Has Taken Off

Raging Calf

Eating Baby (the prequel to 'Bringing up Baby')

Twelve Mildly Irritated Men

Prince Kong

How Green Is My Valley Going to Be?

Kitten on a Hot Tin Roof

F.F. (the prequel to 'Gigi')

Cheese-Based Late Supper on Elm Street

Night of the Living

You Won't Believe What Private Ryan's Gone and Done

The Man Who Knew Enough

Groundhog Day

Robo-Community Support Officer

The Pre-natal Ultimatum

Let's Just Hope No Invaders Snatch These Bodies

The Spy Who Didn't Come In Because It Was Warm Out

Start Up the Khyber

Dr Maybe

I Hope Something Funny Happens on the Way to the Forum

Kramer and Kramer

Now Where's Red October Gone?

Notre Dame Seeks Bellringer

Illegal Immigrant Kane

Dial G for Grievous Bodily Harm

It's a Mad Mad Mad Mad World of Leather

A Cracking Night at Tiffany's

Build Your Wagon

O Brother Don't Go Wandering Off

Apocalypse Soon

Universally Challenged

*This is our version of the great college student TV quiz,
which has been re-titled specially to suit the teams. At
the height of the Cold War, Cambridge University was a
hotbed of intrigue. As a student there in the early 1960s,
Tim Brooke-Taylor was approached by the KGB, who
were looking to recruit an agent to act as a sleeper. They
wanted someone they could rely on to keep a low profile
and do nothing for the next forty or fifty years.*

What is the origin of the
brassiere?

It was invented so night
watchmen could keep their
hands warm

*(It is believed to have been invented
around 2,500 BC on the Greek island
of Crete, where the Minoan women
wore an early version of the modern
bra which lifted the wearer's bare
breasts entirely out of their garments)*

What can you do if you like
cottage pie but are not sure
about the quality of your mince?

Well, you could improve it by
putting one hand on your hip
as you walk about. Try that
and I think you'll find you'll be
the talk of the cottage

*(Mince the leftover meat from a joint
of roast beef. Delicious)*

Why are giant pandas in the zoo so bad at mating?
You're not the first one to have been disappointed. . .
(Female pandas are only receptive to the males for two or three days a year. If the male pandas try at the wrong time, they get bitten)

What's a good way to determine whether an animal is dangerous?
Run towards it, waving your arms in the air. If it backs away, it's not dangerous
(Poking it with a stick is generally considered the most effective way)

How did the expression 'To put a sock in it' originate?
It came from the instruction manual of the world's smallest tumble dryer
(Old-fashioned gramophones had no volume control, so they used to put a sock in the horn)

What's the best thing to do if attacked by an aggressive dog?
Fake an orgasm
(Attempt to force its legs apart sideways: this pulls apart the ribs and causes breathing difficulties)

Why are eggs egg-shaped?
Never mind that – how do hens know the size of egg cups?
(The curve provides the strongest resistance to outside forces)

Why can't you buy tinned bananas?
Because nobody sells them
(It's due to extreme temperatures in the tinning process)

Why do the Chinese eat with chopsticks?
Because a fork's out of the question
(It's because Confucius said they shouldn't use instruments of slaughter at the dining table)

What sport puts the greatest strain on the human body?
Ladies' beach volleyball. Half an hour of watching that and I'm absolutely knackered
(Probably motor racing)

Is it true that men think about sex every eight minutes?
Actually that's a complete phallus – fallacy
(It's never been formally proved)

Why do bras fasten at the back?
If they opened at the front
she wouldn't be able to see the
film properly

(Because at one time all ladies were
dressed by a maid)

What should you do if attacked
by a shark?
Phone Claws Direct

(Keep calm. Maintain eye contact. If
you've got a stick, hold it straight out
towards the shark's eye)

What is the etiquette if you find
you're the first person to arrive
at an organised orgy?
Try and make an entrance

(Shower first, be prompt, bring your
own toys, use only mild dirty talk, and
take care to alternate sexes)

How can you ensure that your
omelettes are really fluffy?
Before cooking, stir in a
couple of hamsters

(Add a squirt of soda water to the egg
mixture before cooking)

How can I ensure my lipstick
lasts longer?
Just do one lip

(Powder your lips before applying the
lipstick)

Why don't dogs need glasses?
Because they can drink
straight from the toilet bowl

(Because for most non-human
mammals the ocular refraction for
optimal distance vision tends strongly
towards emmetropia, or perfect vision)

I'm embarrassed about my short
stumpy legs. Is there any way
I can give the impression of
having longer legs?
Say to people: 'I'm further
away than you think'

(Choose skirts with a slit up the side.
It gives the illusion of length and
slenderness)

I have a large bust and
consequently always wear a bra
for support. If I was flying in
space, would I no longer require
my bra? And, if not, what shape
would my breasts assume?
The brassiere is optional –
just avoid wearing brightly
coloured clothing to prevent
being mistaken for a lava lamp

(The correspondent would probably be
grateful for the use of a bra at blast-
off and re-entry, though she wouldn't
need a bra at zero gravity)

Do giraffes take special precautions during thunderstorms?
Yes – they dash down to the chemist and buy an enormous packet of three
(No)

Is it true that cows sitting down is a portent of rain?
Possibly, but it's not as reliable a portent as a pharmacy full of giraffes
(No)

Why do we tie shoes to the back of the cars of newlyweds?
Because people get upset when you do it to hearses
(From biblical times the shoe has been a sign of ownership – early European parents used to throw shoes at the bride as a renunciation of their authority over her)

My child has chicken pox. Is there anything I can do to make the experience less miserable for him?
Give his sister typhoid
(When it's time to apply the calamine lotion, tip some into a pot and give your child a paintbrush. He'll have great fun in joining the dots)

How can I tell whether the aubergine in my larder is male or female?
If the aubergine is female it says, 'We should really knock this larder through and have a fridge freezer in here.' And then a couple of years later it says, 'You know, things kept much better when we had the old larder.' And then you have to get a new kitchen because the old one doesn't go with the napkin rings
(The male aubergine has fewer seeds and a round shallow indentation on its bottom)

What's the best way to cook a live crab?
Set fire to your knickers
(Place it in cold water and cook on a low heat. If you put it in boiling water its membrane will let in water and its bits will fall off)

Is there any way you can make cheeses live longer in your larder?
Don't worry – cheeses will rise again on the third day
(Put the cheeses in a box and add a sugar cube. This will extend their life)

I'm concerned that my bust is too large. Is there a good way to draw attention away from it?
Yes. Grow a beard

(Wear a very simple plain white shirt)

I have a square face and find buying hats difficult. What do you suggest?
A small cardboard box and a feather

(Buy a wide-brimmed hat. It will suit you best)

Why do women open their mouths when applying mascara?
To say: 'Can you take the steering wheel?'

(There are two central theories. 1. It eliminates blinking – the enemy to successful mascara application. 2. Opening the mouth stretches the skin on the eyeballs, making it easier to apply the mascara)

Why don't women faint as much as they used to?
Because it's not as big as it used to be

(This is probably due to the eradication of the corset, which made it impossible for the wearer to draw a deep breath)

Why do my boxer shorts have straight frontal slits while my underpants have complicated trap doors?
Because it's much harder getting it out with boxing gloves

(Underpants are designed to stretch and boxer shorts are not. Without the trap door underpants would be liable to gape open at unfortunate moments)

Why do zebras have black and white stripes?
It's a barcode so lions know their sell-by date

(The most likely explanation is that it protects them against biting insects such as the tsetse fly)

How would you stop a small dog from yapping?
I've never seen a small dog from Yapping

(Hold it up at arm's length and squirt water in its face)

How can you ensure your pet tarantula will be easy to handle?
Fit it with handles

(Put it in the fridge. After a few minutes its metabolism will slow down)

What's a good way to stop buttons from dropping off?
A banjo duet by the Ugly Sisters usually does the trick
(Dab a drop of clear nail polish onto the thread. This will harden and make it more difficult for the thread to break off)

Do animals or birds ever refer to each other by name?
Yes, but only if they're called Woof, Miaow or Moo.
(No. But some are able to recognise one another. Humph: 'And I know how they do it, the disgusting creatures')

Why do the clergy wear dog collars?
Why does the Archbishop of Canterbury worry sheep?
(A visiting Roman Catholic order first wore them in the 1840s and the look caught on)

What is the origin of the nursery rhyme 'Mary Had a Little Lamb'?
Sellafield Maternity Ward
(It was composed by Mrs Sarah Hale of Boston, after she'd been told of a case in which a pet lamb had followed its young owner to school)

Why do men always do the cooking at barbecues?
Because women are completely incapable of burning meat properly
(It's been suggested that it revives their caveman instincts)

Why did men start shaving?
Because people kept thinking they were folk singers
(It was to prevent an enemy soldier from gaining the advantage by grabbing his opponent by the beard)

Why do washing machines have windows?
It's for the cat to see out of
(It's so you can look inside them without soapy water spilling out onto the floor)

Why do many hotels fold the first piece of toilet paper in the bathroom into a little 'V'?
Because it's too difficult to fold it into the letter 'Q'
(According to the International Association of Holiday Inns, hotels want to give their guests the confidence that their bathroom has been cleaned since the last guest used the room. A 'V' in the loo paper is a clear sign that no one has used the lavatory since the room was last cleaned)

Why were duels always fought at dawn?

Well, one of them had to get to work

(Not all duels were fought at dawn, but most appear to have been. This is probably because fighting a duel at twilight could prove difficult, and also because there would be less chance of interference from the law)

I'm about to do a parachute jump for charity, but I'm disconcerted by the large hole at the top of the parachute. Can you tell me what it's for?

It's an access point for the ambulance crew

(It's called an apex vent. Before it was invented, air used to spill out from either end of the canopy. This is why parachutists during the war used to swing from side to side like a pendulum as they descended)

Is it just coincidence that my finger fits exactly into my nostril?

Yes – in fact it's one of several coincidences

(Natural selection could have played a factor. Females in the Pliocene period might have preferred mating with males who picked their noses, or perhaps males and females picked each other's noses in a courtship ritual. If not, then it probably is just a coincidence)

Does the little dot on an 'i' have a name?

Conjunctivitis

(It's called a tittle)

Celebrity Misquotes

Today, everything on TV is celebrity-driven. I even notice on my pack of breakfast sausages there's a picture of Antony Worrall Thompson. Underneath it says 'prick with a fork'. In this game, the teams are asked to suggest quotations that certain celebrities – alive or dead – would be most unlikely ever to say.

Alexander Graham Bell
It's engaged!

Moses
If they're free – I'll take ten

Winston Churchill
Should Herr Hitler ever set foot on the shores of our beloved country you won't see my baggy striped trousers for dust

Mother Teresa
I was so drunk last night I ended up going home with a couple of sailors

Neil Kinnock
To cut a long story short. . .

Ted Heath
That Margaret Roberts, she looks a bit useful. . .

The Pope
Are you all right for the weekend, sir?

Van Gogh
I want a Walkman for Christmas

Duke of Wellington at Waterloo
Stuff this for a game of soldiers

Michaelangelo
Sorry, I only do floors

Gandhi
'Ere, mush, you trying to be funny?

Mary Whitehouse
I'm a bum and tits woman myself

Jane Austen
I usually write the sex bits first

Jeffrey Archer
Look, in all honesty...

Julius Caesar
Bloody Brutus, I knew you'd be in the thick of it!

William Wordsworth
What rhymes with hills?

The Marquis de Sade
No need to get nasty

Beethoven
There's no need to shout!

The Orange Order
Well, I suppose we don't have to go this way

Marcel Marceau
Hello!

St Paul
I'm sure there's a perfectly rational scientific explanation for it

Frans Hals
Can't you Cavaliers be serious for one moment?

Henry VIII
But I would like to be friends

Bill Clinton
Please! I'm married!

Jonathan Miller
Of course, I'm no expert on the subject

Cliff Richard: 'What do you mean you're pregnant?'

The Duchess of York
No, no, I'll pay!

Jerry Springer
Your private life is no concern of mine

Picasso
Can you see what it is yet?

The Queen
We couldn't give a toss

Duke of Edinburgh
Far be it from me to comment

Richard Littlejohn
Well, I'd need to give that some thought before I express an opinion

Neil and Christine Hamilton
Oh we couldn't do that

Laurence Llewellyn-Bowen
Does this make me look a bit camp?

David Attenborough
No, pass me the BIG gun

King Harold
20/20, me

Jeremy Hardy
And now here's a song you'll all recognise

David Starkey
Where are my manners?

Queen Victoria
I pissed myself

Barry Cryer
No thanks, I've already had a half

Tim Brooke-Taylor
No, I'll get them in

Charlie Dimmock
Gosh. It lifts and separates

John Humphrys
No, no, please finish your point

Long John Silver
I'll take the pair

Martin Luther
I'll just pop these under the door

Boutros Boutros-Ghali
Oh, so you're called Boutros Boutros as well?

Nicholas Parsons
Oh, you don't want me in the photograph

Henry VIII
You know what they say – once a Catholic. . .

John Prescott
In a word. . .

Stephen Fry
I haven't the faintest idea

Vinnie Jones
Of course theatre's my first love

Boardo Nouveau

AT THE HAYMARKET THEATRE

CHAIR   Of all the board games you hear played on the radio, there's none that compares with our very own compendium of fun: 'Boardo'. The most popular gaming elements are gathered together here, making this the perfect way to fill a boring afternoon. We're now going to play the new, recently updated and excitingly improved version. So, stand by for a round of 'Boardo Nouveau'. And without further ado, who's Blue?

TIM   That's me.

VICTORIA   I'm Yellow.

GRAEME   I'm Green.

CHAIR   Barry, are you Red?

BARRY   Yes.

CHAIR   So you should be – now zip it up and let's get on with the game. Have you selected your tokens?

GRAEME   I've got a little top hat.

TIM   I didn't realise there was a dress code.

BARRY   I wanted the top hat. Well then, I'll take the little racing car.

VICTORIA   I suppose being a girl I ought to be either the iron or the thimble. So I'll choose. . . the Kalashnikov.

CHAIR   And Tim?

TIM   I'm a little teapot.

CHAIR   Of course you are. Then let Boardo commence.

BARRY   I'm sitting to the right of the dealer so I'll start. (Dice rattle and throw) Four. (Four board thumps) Fleet Street. . . Leicester Square. . . Piccadilly. . . Waterworks!

CHAIR   Well, hurry back. Victoria, you'd better start.

VICTORIA   Luck be a lady tonight. . . (Dice rattle and throw) Double six! Do I get another throw?

CHAIR   Yes, you do.

VICTORIA   (Dice rattle and throw) Oh. Three.

TIM   Should have stuck with double six.

VICTORIA   (Three board thumps) Wormwood Scrubs.

TIM   Look, your second W is on a triple letter score.

VICTORIA   So that's four points.

CHAIR   And that means you can either have a green wedge for Science and Nature or you can have a house.

VICTORIA   I think I'll have a house please.

            (FX: Cash register – Ker-ching!)

VICTORIA   Ooh, a semi!

GRAEME   OK. (Dice rattle and throw) Woah! Seventeen the hard way! (Two heavy board thumps) This top hat is heavier than it looks. (Thump!)

(FX: Cat screech)

GRAEME   Right, near enough. I'll put a little house here. No, not a house. . . no, a hotel. . . no. I'll put up a cathedral.

(FX: Cash register – Ker-ching! Ker-ching! Ker-ching!)

(MUSIC: Organ chord)

TIM   My throw, I believe. (Dice rattle and throw) Five. (Five board thumps) Cricklewood Lane. Ah this one's free so I think I shall erect. . . an Erotic Gherkin.

(FX: Cash register – Ker-ching! Ker-ching! Ker-ching! Ker-ching! Ker-ching! Ker-ching! Ker-ching!)

BARRY   I'm back.

CHAIR   Ah, Barry, it's your turn.

BARRY   OK. (Rummages in Scrabble bag and throws down seven letters) Q but no U. . . hmm. . . T. . . E. . . oh yes, I can spell 'Three'! (Twelve board thumps) Oh damn, I've landed on a snake! So that takes me down to. . . this ladder. Up I go to. . . ah, Chance Card. Let's see: 'Golden handshake. Collect two hundred. . . thousand. . . million pounds from each player.' So hand it over!

(FX: Rifle shot)

BARRY   Missed!

CHAIR   That'll do, Victoria! It's the thimble for you, young lady!

VICTORIA   Oh all right. (Dice rattle and throw) Clickety-click. One! What do I do now?

TIM   Black ten on the red Jack.

VICTORIA   Good thinking. Checkmate!

GRAEME   I don't think so! (Dice rattle and throw) Queen's Bishop to Old Kent Road. (Board thump)

TIM   You've landed on my Gherkin.

GRAEME   I do apologise. I didn't notice.

TIM   They never do.

BARRY   Excuse me. How long is this supposed to take?

CHAIR   It says on the box: 'Five to seven years.'

VICTORIA   It certainly seems like it.

CHAIR   Tim, your go.

TIM   OK!

           (FX: Tennis service. Distant cry
           of 'Out!')

CHAIR   Second serve.

VICTORIA   Come on, Tim!

TIM   What's the score?

CHAIR   Fifteen, love.

TIM   Thanks, darling. Here goes. . . (Dice rattle and throw)
           (Board thumps) Chance! (Card dealt) Aha! Mrs Bun
           the butcher's son. Go direct to jail. Do not pass water.

VICTORIA   Oh bad luck, Tim!

BARRY   Is it me?

GRAEME   Well, it wasn't me.

BARRY   Right. (Dice rattle and throw) Three. (Board thumps)
           Pool Street Station.

CHAIR   Sorry, there's no such place.

BARRY   There is if you take the Liver out of it.

GRAEME   Need a steady hand for that. . .
           (FX: Electric buzz from Operation game)

BARRY   Blast!

CHAIR   Go back two spaces.

BARRY   (Board thumps) Park Lane.

TIM   Gotcha! Ha ha! You owe me rent! I've got twenty-eight hotels on Park Lane.

CHAIR   Actually I think you're only supposed to have twenty-seven.

TIM   Damn. I'd better remove one from the stack.

VICTORIA   Yes. Carefully remove one from the stack of hotels. . .

TIM   I'll just ease this one. . .

VICTORIA   No, go for the one on the other side!

TIM   Let me do it my way. Easy does it. . .

           (FX: Jenga Tumbling Tower – wood blocks collapse followed by desk falling apart, then building collapses, crashing walls, splintering beams, clanging girders, finally tumbling into rubble [very long])

TIM   Oops.

CHAIR   Never mind, it still works as an outdoor game. Victoria, carry on.

VICTORIA   (Dice rattle and throw) Two fat ladies, number five! (Thump thump thump thump. Bath splash!) Oh! Damn! OK, I suspect Colonel Mustard in the bath with Miss Scarlet. And the inflatable candlestick.

CHAIR	Don't be silly. And at this stage of the game I have to tell you that Graeme and Barry are £220 ahead, so Tim and Victoria, you are losing badly. And you know what that means. . .
	(MUSIC: Prokoviev's 'Romeo and Juliet')
CHAIR	Yes, it's time to step into the Boardo-room. Good morning, everybody.
ALL	Good morning, Sue Ellen.
CHAIR	And don't call me Sue Ellen. Right, Tim and Victoria – who was your project leader?
VICTORIA	Tim was, Sue Ellen.
CHAIR	Tim, you was, was you?
TIM	Yes, Sue Ellen.
CHAIR	Right. Good team leader was he?
VICTORIA	Dreadful. Absolutely hopeless. He was an utter disgrace, Sue Ellen.
CHAIR	So, Tim. Why shouldn't I fire you?
TIM	I'm cute, Sue Ellen.
CHAIR	That's true. Well, are there any other Tims here in the audience? You? You're a Tim too? Well, you're not cute, so Tim in the audience – you're fired!
	(MUSIC: Prokoviev's 'Romeo and Juliet' ending)

DO-IT-YOURSELF
Song Book

Midnight Drain to Georgia

B & Q and Q & B and Q for You and B for Me

IKEA and Tina Turner singing 'River Deep MFI'

You Screw Something for Me and I'll Screw Something for You

I'm Putting on My Top Coat

I DIY, I Don't Know Why I Do

If a Pickaxe Paints a Thousand Words

'We Are Nailing' by Dynorod Stewart

Consider Your Shelves Well Up

Singing Polyfilla Doodle All the Day

Touch Me Up in the Morning

Flat Pack All Your Cares and Woes

U-bend Me Shake Me Any Way You Want Me

Knowing Me, Knowing Glue

Viva Espanner

The Stripper

Making Good Is Hard to Do

I've Got You Under My Skip

Twist and Grout

Undercoat Overcoat

Tack My Bitch Up

Da Doo Ronseal

White Spirit in the Sky

Socket Man

The Kids Araldite

Hard-hatted Hannah

Return to Render

Got Myself a Swirling, Twirling,
Thrilling, Drilling Cordless Drill

A You're Adjustable, B Cos
You're a Wrench

You Know You Make Me Wanna
Grout (sung by Hinge and
Bracket)

Slap My Bitumen Up

Bradawl Be the Day

Cisterns Are Doing It for
Themselves

AND FOR WHEN YOU GET THE BUILDERS IN

The First Quote Is the Cheapest

Tomorrow, Tomorrow, I'll Be
There Tomorrow

Whip Crack Away – or just
leave it hanging out of your
trousers

It's My Putty and I'll Cry if I
Want To

Gazetteer

PART 4

SOUTHAMPTON

The jewel of England's ferry ports

SOUTHAMPTON is the gateway to the New Forest. In the year 1100, King William Rufus was killed there by an arrow while out hunting. Historians believe William was assassinated as he was so unpopular with the barons. One who dared to criticise the King was the Earl of Northumbria, so William had him castrated, after which he spoke of the King really quite highly.

Another theory is that William Rufus was hated because he never married and produced no children and so it was simply homophobia on the part of the Norman Barons. That kind of prejudice is detestable. Typical French.

The New Forest is home to a new organisation founded by Sir David Attenborough and Dame Jane Goodall, which campaigns against the exploitation of chimpanzees. However, when they moved into their new premises, they struggled to get a piano down the stairs before throwing buns at each other over tea.

It was in Southampton that the Pilgrim Fathers' ship, the 'Mayflower', was built. The vessel set sail in 1620 with a group of yeomen and landed gentry, which was a surprise as they were actually fishing for haddock.

At a memorable Sunday-afternoon concert in 1945, Ted and Barbara Andrews introduced their ten-year-old daughter Julie on the stage of Southampton's

Empire Theatre. She stood on a box and began to sing, and we all know what happened to young Miss Andrews after that: she was rubbish, so she went into the family liver salts business.

As transatlantic liners grew ever bigger, in 1932 Southampton City Council commissioned the civil engineer Albert Peterson, who built them the world's largest dry dock. So they sacked him and got someone to build one that had water in it.

At the nearby National Motor Museum is the original million-pound James Bond Aston Martin DB4, which can throw an oil slick and a massive smokescreen out of the back. Alternatively, there's a 1982 Vauxhall Cavalier on eBay that will do that for £125.

TAUNTON

Undisputed county town of Somerset

TAUNTON was initially established as a centre of trade based around its seaport and docks, but seafaring traders were reluctant to land there as not only were excise import dues higher than elsewhere, but it was also sixteen miles from the nearest coast.

Industry in Taunton only really took off with the completion of the Kennet and Avon Canal in 1810. Taunton Museum displays pictures of heavily laden barges drawn by horses. How they trained horses to hold pencils remains a mystery.

Useful rare minerals found in the area include kaolin and flint glass, which were essential for making fine lenses for optical instruments. These include the actual telescope Nelson famously used when he said: 'I see no ship', before he walked straight into the side of HMS 'Victory', and took his left eye out.

The nearby Creech St Michael Miniature Railway boasts the smallest train carriages in England, with passengers often sitting on each other's laps or hanging their legs over the shoulders of the person in front. These perfect, tiny models of real carriages are generously on loan from Virgin Trains.
Early drafts of the ever-popular children's stories of 'Winnie the Pooh' were written here by A. A. Milne, just before he

started his breakdown recovery service.

Frome was the birthplace of Formula One racing driver Jenson Button. He recently returned to be granted the freedom of the city by the Lady Mayor. In celebration, he picked her up, shook her by the neck and threw her over the crowd.

Nearby Norton Fitzwarren is the summer home of the American novelist Lionel Shriver whose real name is Margaret Ann Shriver. Noted for her novel 'We Need to Talk About Kevin', Shriver decided to use a man's name when she began writing because she wanted to be taken seriously. That's so cute.

The film actress Jenny Agutter was born in Taunton. Movie connoisseurs consider many of her early films worth seeing over and again, including 'Walkabout', 'Equus' and 'An American Werewolf in London'. Miss Agutter also made some other films where she doesn't get her kit off, apparently.

WARWICK

County town of Warwickshire

WHEN the Romans arrived in this area in AD 52, they discovered a tribe of cannibals. Following a short battle, a truce was called and the Legionnaire Tiberium was invited to discuss peace terms over a feast. However, he got cold feet, so he sent them back.

The exiled ruler of the northern kingdom, Mary, Queen of Scots was incarcerated in Warwick Castle before being beheaded by order of her cousin, Elizabeth I, as she insisted she be Queen of the South. That's when they took a game of Subbuteo really seriously.

In 1487, the Honourable Guild of Glaziers was established in Warwick to train apprentice boys in the craft of glass-making and window construction, with some taken so young they first had go through putty training.

Warwick School claims to be the oldest boys' school in Britain. It's surprising how smart a school cap, blazer and short trousers look on a thirty-seven-year-old.

Warwick University boasts a renowned faculty of archaeology, whose scientists recently set about locating the lost city of Atlantis. The head of department was sadly forced to miss the first sailing of their exploration vessel when he was delayed, unable to find his car keys.

When it opened in 1924, the Warwick Grand Empire Hotel employed page boys who wore pill box hats and jackets with brass buttons. Then, following complaints, they gave them trousers.

It was at the Warwick Counselling Centre that the pioneering therapist Dr James Barfield repeatedly tried, but failed, to launch a self-harming awareness group. He said it was like banging his head against a brick wall.

Warwick is home to the Midlands Museum of Historic Photography. However, a recent exhibition of black-and-white magazine prints of 1950s naturists was closed down following a complaint from the images' copyright owners. Disappointed visitors described

the decision as 'Health and Efficiency gone mad'.

Nearby Leamington Spa is where lawn tennis is regulated and administered. Broadcast matters are also covered, and in 2009 the Leamington Committee was called to meet following complaints over the way TV camera angles were looking up lady players' skirts. Consequently, the cameras were lowered to give a better view.

In Priory Road, there's a blue plaque on the house of Fred Harrison, the father of modern ventriloquism, who died there in 1957. This is despite his death-bed wish: 'Glease, glease, don't gut a glue glaque on my gungalow.'

WATFORD

Near the M25

THE first recorded mention of the name 'Watford' in print was in the town's Anglo-Saxon charter of 1042. The second was this one.

Watford's Cassiobury Park was for centuries the seat of the Earls of Essex, and in

1536, hosted a banquet for Henry VIII. A huge boar was slaughtered and cooked in the grand hall. It was ordered that every part be cooked as delicacies, including the ears, nose and tail, boiled, or roasted whole. Due to a slight misunderstanding, the chef found several diners sending back his roasted hole.

The original grand house at Cassiobury was built in the fourteenth century by the first Earl of Essex, but in 1987, after six centuries of occupation by the Essex family, the house was renovated by experts who spent seven years carefully cleaning layers of peroxide and fake tan from the walls.

In the 1650s, Abbots Langley was the home of Thomas Greenhill, a pioneer in the art of embalming who became so skilled he was invited to embalm the seventh Duke of Norfolk. Greenhill plugged all the main orifices with saltpeter-soaked corks, before filling the body with a mixture of methanol and linseed oil through a funnel hammered into the nose. The Duke said it was so painful he almost wished he was dead.

Thomas Greenhill's mother, Elizabeth, bore thirty-eight other children. Mrs Greenhill explained her phenomenal fecundity as a result of neither smoking nor drinking and living on a diet of stale carrots, limp lettuce and cabbage stalks.

During the Second World War, the de Havilland Aircraft factory was based at Leavesden Aerodrome. Leavesden was the home of the Halifax bomber, the notorious building society saboteur.

The only Englishman to become Pope, Adrian VI, was born Nicholas Breakspear near Watford in 1100. He came from a brewing family, at a time when beer was the staple drink with every meal. Even in the Vatican, it was said Pope Adrian couldn't enjoy his breakfast without a Bishop's Finger inside him.

Famous local Watford names include Andrew Ridgeley, who formed one half of the 1980s pop duo Wham! with George Michael. When the pair were reunited recently, fans gathered outside a restaurant to watch as Ridgeley stepped from his car and went through the door, while George Michael did it the other way round.

Local man Fred Housego won 'Mastermind' in 1980. The London cabbie from Croxley passed on only one question, which was: 'In monetary terms, what is the meaning of the word "change"?'

The former Spice Girl Emma Bunton lives nearby. Emma left the group in 1999 to become a former Spice Girl.

ENCLUEDOPAEDIA BRITANNICA

Seventeen things you never knew about the people and places of the British Isles

THE artist George Stubbs, who was born in Lancashire in 1724, began painting horses when he was just seven years old. When his mother saw what he'd done, Stubbs was made to clean the horses up with turps, give them a lump of sugar and was sent to bed early with no supper.

Alan Turing, the wartime Enigma code-breaker, spent his last years near Northampton. The mathematician, logician, master cryptanalyst and computer scientist was a keen motorist, but never drove in the town, as he couldn't work out how to get round the one-way system.

Ashford, in Middlesex, is home to the British Literacy Skills Research Facility. In 2011, its senior practitioner, Dr James Holland, was awarded an oboe for his work on dyslexia.

St Pancras Railway Station in west London is named after the first-century Greek who travelled to Jerusalem during the earthly ministry of Jesus; was baptised in Antioch; withdrew to a cave in Pontus where he was discovered by St Peter; was sent to Sicily where he met his death by stoning at the hands of pagan opponents of the new religion; and is the patron saint of replacement bus services.

The explorer Edward Fitzsimmonds was born in Bushey, Hertfordshire, in 1874, the son of a wealthy merchant. Over a period of thirty years, Fitzsimmonds spent his family fortune funding repeated searches for the magnetic South

Pole, and then found it stuck on the fridge door.

In 2008, the village of Lunt in Merseyside was plagued by vandals constantly changing their road signs to read as a rude word. Consequently, the parish council agreed to change the name, and it's since been known as the village of Locksucker.

The University of Lancaster mathematics professor Alan Dobson wrote the definitive work on the life of Euclid of Alexandria (325–265 BC), the father of modern geometry. Dobson uncovered many fascinating aspects of Euclid's private life. Apparently conducting simultaneous affairs with a dozen women, Euclid was said to be in a love dodecahedron.

Britain's first-ever industrial injury claim was filed in 1872 by Joseph Mitchell of Sheffield. Mr Mitchell's claim was successful but he never lived to receive his compensation as he died the day the five-week hearing ended. His family said Mr Mitchell, a tanner who had fallen into a vat of hot goose grease, gently slipped away.

When Ordnance Survey maps were first drawn in the nineteenth century, bored surveyors put in jokes. In Lincolnshire there's a contour line in the shape of a baby elephant, and in Essex there's the outline of a little toilet: Romford.

The standardisation of time measurement was defined by the Horological Synod of Sidcup in 1406, which decreed that a year would comprise 365 units of twenty-four hours each, but couldn't agree what this twenty-four-hour unit should be named. After three weeks of constant debate, the synod members became tired and decided to call it a day.

The ornate clock on Shepton Mallet town hall was made by John 'Longitude' Harrison of Wakefield in 1713. The precision timepiece has a double escapement moon phase movement which every twenty-eight days reveals a large bare arse.

New Church of England holy days, which became 'holidays', were calendarised by the Diet of Stamford in 1542 as part of the process of the English Reformation. These new religious feasts included Shrove Tuesday, Good Friday, Ash Wednesday, Sheffield Wednesday, Man Friday, Robin Day, Darren Day and Chocolate Ice Cream Sunday.

Until 1898, at Oxford University, women students were only allowed to attend their own colleges. The first to break with this tradition was Katherine Palmer-Green, who was accepted to study mine engineering. Miss Palmer-Green was soon playing for her college cricket side, gained a winner's medal in the boat race, became a boxing blue, and then, in 1902, was awarded 'Pipe Smoker of the Year'.

St Michael's Mount is a tidal island located 366 metres off the Mount's Bay coast of Cornwall. The name derives from the monastery that was there until the eleventh century, dedicated to St Michael, the patron saint of returned cardigans.

Britain's first motor show was organised by the Society of Motor Manufacturers and Traders and was held at Crystal Palace, London, in 1903. How visitors gasped in amazement when the Rover Company's latest steam-driven, coal-fired, seven-mile-an-hour, wood-and-canvas-bodied car was unveiled in 1986.

The county of Gloucestershire is the world centre of the manufacturing of aviation precision instruments and controls by firms such as Smiths Industries and Dowty. A systems programme is currently being developed there, that might one day calculate how a Ryanair flight advertised at £4.99 actually costs £175, or £225 if you want a seat.

The first cine camera in Britain was built by Henry Fox Talbot of London. In 1876, he took the first-ever moving pictures of traffic in Edgware Road. Coincidentally, also the last.

SWEET-TOOTHED
Film Club

24-Hour Smartie People

Yankee Doodle Candy

KitKat on a Hot Tin Roof

Stanley Kubrick's 'A Chocolate Orange'

The Bournville Ultimatum

The Munch of the Penguins

Follow That Caramel

Galaxy Quest

Petit Four Horsemen of the Apocalypse

Kung Fu Pain-au-Chocolat

Hello Lolly

Days of Wine Gums and Cadbury's Roses

Marathon Man (remade as 'Snickers Man')

Sex, Drugs and Rock and Rolos

Dial M for Werthers

The Guns of Toblerone

Priscilla, Queen of the Dessert

Custard's Last Stand

Welcome Back to the Five and Dime Bar, Jimmy Dean, Jimmy Dean

Bad Day at Blackpool Rock

The Adventures of Sherbet Holmes

Battle of the Little Cream Horn

The Wind that Shakes the Barley Sugars

V for Vienetta

Spotted Dick Tracey

I'm All Right, Flapjack

Wall's Treat

McVitie Vitie Bang Bang

The Penguin Has Landed

Paint Your Wagon Wheel

J.R.R. Tolkien's 'The Hobnob'

Butch Cassidy and the Milky Bar Kid

Local Aero

The Horse Whispa

Around the Twirl in Eighty Days

Oliver Twix

Terry's All Goldfinger

Gone in Sixty Seconds, but very tasty

Terry's Clockwork Orange

Bring Me the Cream Egg of Alfredo Garcia

Mutiny on the Bounty

Rolo Cop

The Unbearable Lightness of Maltesers

No Crunchie for Old Men

The Twirl with the Dragon Tattoo

Dirty Haribo

Bendicks Like Beckham

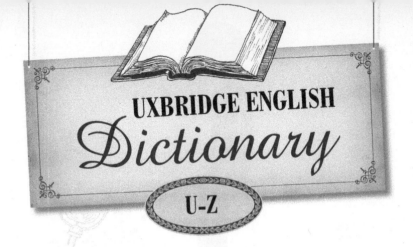

UXBRIDGE ENGLISH
Dictionary

U-Z

Umbrage
Card game for the hesitant

Unfettered
Without Greek cheese

Urinate
You're a size eight

Vanish
Rather like a van

Varicose
Nearby

Fig.18. Urinate

Walnut
An obsessive bricklayer

Warehouse
A person who turns into a house at the full moon

Fig.19. Wikileaks

Website
The distance between a web and the ground

Wince
A setting on Jonathan Ross's washing machine

Wikileaks
What happens when you use a basket as a urinal

Woodpecker
Low cost penis replacement

Welfare
Blonde, innit

Why-aye
Geordie broadband

X-ray
Former fish

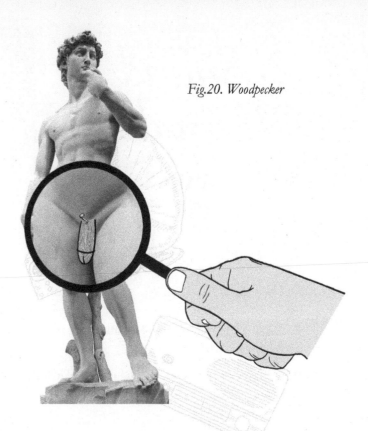

Fig.20. Woodpecker

Yacht
A negative yes

Yodelling
Trainee Jedi knight

Zinc
To zubside beneath the zea

Zip-a-dee-doo-dah
Your flies are undone

Zucchini
Animal park enthusiast

Sound Charades

PART 2

TV PROGRAMME: *Three Words*

BOY   'Ere, Dad. The kids at school say that your sister Muriel played for Arsenal.

DAD   Well, they're right, Gavin, she did indeed play for Arsenal.

BOY   I can't believe that, Dad.

DAD   It may be hard to believe, but let me prove it to you. Have a look at what I've got here in this drawer. . . Look at these.

BOY   Gosh!

DAD   Yes, they're strong you see – reinforced gusset, a go-faster flap and a little Arsenal logo on the leg.

BOY   What's a gusset, Dad?

DAD   He's a rugby player, I believe.

(Auntie's Sporting Bloomers)

TWO FILMS: *One Word*

DOCTOR	Good morning, how's the patient today?
CONSULTANT	Not very well, I'm afraid.
DOCTOR	What!? But He's the Supreme Being, the Creator of the World.
CONSULTANT	That's as may be, but he fell ill yesterday, and today he's worse.

(Godzilla)

FILM: *One Word*

MAN 1	(Clearly in some discomfort) Excuse me, I wonder if you could help me?
MAN 2	Ah yes. Turn left at the elephant house, cross over by the penguins, carry on past the lions' cage and it's third on your right.
MAN 1	Thank you very much.

(Zulu)

TV PROGRAMME: *One Word*

DOUGAL	Ah, Hamish!
HAMISH	You'll have had your tea, Dougal. . .
DOUGAL	Aye, yes. What's the time, by the way?
FX	WOOF! WOOF! WOOF!
HAMISH	Three o'clock.

DOUGAL   Jings! Your sleeve was barking!

HAMISH   Not my sleeve, Dougal, but. . . THIS!

DOUGAL   By the beard of Moira Anderson!!

HAMISH   No thank you, I've got one already.

DOUGAL   What is that strapped to your wrist?

HAMISH   It's a wee chihuahua.

DOUGAL   And it tells the time?

HAMISH   Aye, Dougal, it does. And its movement is guaranteed.

DOUGAL   Rolex?

HAMISH   No no, he's been to the vet.

DOUGAL   And what is this canine chronometer called?

   (Watchdog)

BOOK AND FILM: *Three Words*

HAMISH   Hello, Dougal. Oh, I see you've got your family with you.

DOUGAL   Oh aye, Hamish, I've brought the bairns. Here's wee Victoria. Say hello to Uncle Hamish. And there's wee Euston.

HAMISH   I think I've met this wee soul Paddington. I think I recognise him.

DOUGAL   King's Cross and Liverpool Street are at home just now.

HAMISH   Oh, I did hear that your good lady was expecting.

DOUGAL   Oh aye, that's true, she's twenty minutes overdue.

   (The Railway Children)

FILM: *Two Words*

MAN 1   Which of you fat bastards did this to my camel?

MAN 2   It wasn't me. It must have been done by a straw.

MAN 1   It was you getting on the camel. Climbing onto it. It was the act of getting onto an animal to ride it.

MAN 2   This isn't really about camels, is it?

MAN 1   No. Not really.

(Brokeback Mountain)

BOOK AND FILM: *Two Words*

HAMISH   Ah, Dougal. You'll have had your tea.

DOUGAL   Ooh, I can see you're having your festive lunch.

HAMISH   Pull up a kilt and sit down.

DOUGAL   Oh thank you. Oh my word! What a magificent bird! It's not a turkey, is it?

HAMISH   Oh no, it's not a turkey.

DOUGAL   Pheasant?

HAMISH   No, it's no' a pheasant.

DOUGAL   McNugget?

HAMISH   No, no. This is unique. It's a rare cross. The result of a grouse – a grouse, mark you – mating with a wee finch.

DOUGAL   Jings! That's a one-off.

HAMISH   Aye. That's just what the finch said.

DOUGAL   Poor wee soul. It brings the tears to your eyes. What do you call it – a frouse?

HAMISH   Oh no. No, no, no. Quite the reverse.

(The Grinch)

FILM: *Two Words*

MAN   Potter!

BOY   Yes, sir?

MAN   Don't do that.

BOY   Sorry, sir.

(Dirty Harry)

FILM: *Four Words*

MAN 1   Excuse me, garçon?

MAN 2   Monsieur?

MAN 1   I've tried every bar and brasserie in this city.

MAN 2   For what would zat be, monsieur?

MAN 1   I want a can of fizzy orange juice.

MAN 2   Ah monsieur. Je suis désolé. We have run out of your curious oh-so-English fizzy orange drink. Zere has been a terrific insatiable demand.

MAN 1   Oh, that is a shame.

MAN 2   Ah. I speak to you a lie. We have just one left. Would you like her?

MAN 1   Merci, monsieur. Just what I wanted.

(Last Tango in Paris)

FILM: *Three Words*

VOICE 1   Would you like some more, Field Marshal?

VOICE 2   No thank you, I've had quite enough.

(The Full Monty)

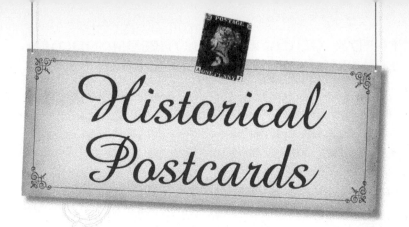

Historical Postcards

The first-ever postcards are believed to have originated in Ancient Egypt. Back then, before the advent of daily newspapers, or indeed written language itself, news of major events was written in the form of hieroglyphs. And if ever there was any news not concerning a bird, a cat, a big eye, and man in a skirt and wimple doing an impression of a teapot, the Egyptians never reported it.

YOUNG DAVID FROM THE HOLY LAND

Big fight with Goliath scheduled for tomorrow. You probably heard about the ruckus at the weigh-in. I've pretty much mastered the stone-slinging business, but just in case, I've positioned Shadrach, Meshach and Abednego on the grassy knoll.

NELSON TO LADY HAMILTON FROM TRAFALGAR

Having a great time at Trafalgar – apart from the pigeons. Captain Hardy has shown me great loyalty and affection, though I still have to remind him `no tongues`. Can't wait to be back with you – hope the eye and the arm are enough to be going on with.

LORD RAGLAN FROM THE CRIMEA

Lost the Light Brigade today, which was a pity. Good news – Lord Cardigan is designing a new uniform. All very hush hush, but Captain Pipe and Colonel Slippers are helping.

CAPTAIN COOK FROM BOTANY BAY

Dear Sir,
Have introduced cricket to the Aborigines. Close of play on first day: England all out 48, Aborigines 743 for 2. Have you thought of turning Yorkshire into a penal settlement?

MARQUIS DE SADE FROM CALAIS TO HIS WIFE

Hotel terrible. Food awful. Weather appalling. Do join me.

CAPTAIN COOK FROM SYDNEY BAY

Dear James,
Counting every minute. Sydney.

LOT FROM SODOM & GOMORRAH

The people here are very free and easy. We've been enjoying the nightlife and no mistake. Sadly they start demolition tomorrow so we'll have to leave. Still, as the wife says, it'll be something to look back on.

ISAAC NEWTON, THE GAZEBO, FRIDAY

Disregard the story in the tabloids. It was Granny Smith who hit me on the head. Nevertheless you'll appreciate the gravity of the situation.

WILLIAM WORDSWORTH, HOLIDAY INN, WINDERMERE

Still can't crack the poem about the host of mouldy espadrilles. Got writer's block. Tried to think of the right word for two weeks. Then I thought, `fortnight', that's it.

RENÉ DESCARTES FROM ANTWERP

Having a wonderful time I think – therefore I am.

SAMUEL MORSE

Dear Dot, must dash.

SHERPA TENZING FROM EVEREST

Reached the top safely. Hillary says I'm to be given the greatest honour. They're going to name a van after me.

NIETZSCHE, SOUTH OF FRANCE

Nice nice. Niece here. Nietzsche.

FROM POMPEII

Vesuvius erupted last night. We were all petrified.

DR LIVINGSTONE FROM AFRICA TO HIS WIFE

Stanley arrived yesterday. Seemed a bit presumptious.

FROM THE THREE WISE MEN IN BETHLEHEM

Off to see new Messiah who's just been born. Bit of a bummer what with it all happening on Christmas Day.

PAUL/SAUL FROM DAMASCUS ADDRESSED TO SOME FRIENDS IN CORINTH

Having a blinding time. Long letter to follow.

FROM MRS JULIUS CAESAR IN DISNEYLAND

Dear Caez,
Place full of ghastly children. Wish you were Herod.

FROM FLORENCE NIGHTINGALE IN CRIMEA

Dear Matron. All a terrible mistake. In my letter I said I wanted to go to the cinema.

DR LIVINGSTONE IN THE CONGO

Dear All,
What a laugh this is. Stanley turned up again today. This time I hid behind the mud huts.

BEETHOVEN TO HIS AGENT

Regarding my next commission – have you heard anything?

JANE AUSTEN TO MOTHER

Publisher loves `Pride and Prejudice' but says all the f-ing and blinding has to go.

SITTING BULL TO CUSTER

Fancy bringing the lads over for a darts match?

KIPLING FROM INDIA

Weather exceedingly good. Beaches exceedingly good. Nightlife exceedingly good. Cake crap.

KING HAROLD IN HASTINGS

Hastings lovely. Looking forward to the big day. Not sure if we should have booked the Red Arrows.

HANNIBAL FROM THE ALPS

This is the last time I charter a jumbo from Virgin.

FROM GEORGE STEPHENSON ON THE 'ROCKET', ON INAUGURAL TRIP FROM STOCKTON TO DARLINGTON

Hi. I'm on the train. I'll talk to you later.

JULIUS CAESAR TO HIS WIFE PORTIA FROM LONDINIUM

Hail Portia. Vici, vidi, veni – or vice versa. Status quo good, Beatles better. Hail and Pace. Julius

CAPTAIN SCOTT FROM THE ANTARCTIC

The weather's not up to much. Catering poor. Oates is just popping out to post this now.

GEOFFREY CHAUCER FROM CANTERBURY

Glenn the Miller's gone missing.

NEVILLE CHAMBERLAIN FROM MUNICH TO MRS CHAMBERLAIN

Weather good. Hitler charming. Piece of paper follows.

MICHELANGELO FROM THE SISTINE CHAPEL

Working flat out. Pope now wants something more like the opening titles to the `South Bank Show'. Am in agony, but the ecstasy keeps me going.

WINSTON CHURCHILL FROM ADMIRALTY HOUSE

Dear Bomber Harris,
Surprised to hear you're planning to bomb Dresden. I said destroy the enemy's armament factories, not their ornament factories.

JOAN OF ARC FROM ORLEANS

Dear Mum,
The Dauphin has booked me a gig at Rouen. Hope he's right about the warm welcome.

MRS BEETHOVEN TO LUDWIG FROM BADEN BADEN

Having a lovely time. Wish you could hear.

EVE TO ADAM

Is there someone else?

FROM JONAH

Having a whale of a time. Gut feeling it's not going to last.

Learn To Play
The Kazoo
My Way!

IN LESS THAN ONE MONTH!

THE HISTORY OF THE KAZOO

The humble kazoo is a type of mirliton – an instrument which employs a vibrating membrane to modify the human voice. Closely related to the eunuch flute, or onion flute (flûte eunuque, flûte à l'oignon and Zwiebelflöte), these members of the woodwind family have been around since the sixteenth and seventeenth centuries, although similar devices have been used in Africa for hundreds of years to disguise the voice or to imitate animals, often for ceremonial purposes.

The modern kazoo, modelled on these early instruments, was developed in the nineteenth century by an African American named Alabama Vest in Macon, Georgia, USA. The first kazoo was manufactured to Vest's specifications by Thaddeus von Clegg, a German clockmaker in Macon. Vest's invention was launched at the Georgia State Fair in 1852 and metal kazoos were first manufactured in Eden, New York, where they are still made to this day in the original factory.

PLAY THE KAZOO – 'A TUNE A DAY'!

Blowing into your kazoo will not produce the typical chirpy rasp we have all come to love so well. Humming will not do, either. The instrument works by imparting its unmistakable 'buzzing' timbral quality to a player's voice only when vocalised into.

Sing 'do do do' into the mouthpiece and you will be amazed to hear the familiar tone emerge. Now all you have to do is to 'do do do' a tune and you too will be a qualified kazooist!

THE KAZOO RECORD

On 3 April 2008, at the Hammersmith Apollo, London, the audience of the live tour of 'I'm Sorry I Haven't a Clue' attempted to break the record for the largest mass kazoo performance with 3,550 people taking part. However, before 'The Guiness Book of Records' could verify the 'Clue' record, on 2 July 2008, an Evangelical Free Church of America Youth Conference in Salt Lake City, Utah, USA, took the Guinness World Record with 5,300 buzzing 'Amazing Grace' for five minutes. What a treat that must have been.

Complete Rhymes

The first nursery rhymes were an early form of public
information warning. It is well documented that 'Ring
a ring a roses, A pocket full of posies' is in fact about
the Black Death of 1348. Other rhymes of the period
included the less well-known warning of rabies arriving
from France: 'Woof, Woof, from the south, We go frothy
at the mouth'; and the graphic description of leprosy:
'Sneeze, sneeze, cough, cough, I see your nose has fallen
off'. Here are some other well-known children's rhymes
the teams were given to finish off.

Ride a cock horse to Banbury Cross
To see a fine lady on a white horse. . .
With rings on her navel and studs on her lip
Who'd have thought nipple rings would ever be hip?

Little Boy Blue, come blow your horn. . .
You must be very supple

Hey diddle-diddle, the cat and the fiddle
The cow jumped over the moon
The little dog laughed to see such sport. . .
And scored some more stuff on a spoon

Little Miss Muffet sat on a tuffet
Eating her curds and whey
There came a big spider
Who sat down beside her. . .
At least he said he was a spider. . .

Old King Cole was a merry old soul
And a merry old soul was he,
He called for his pipe and he called for his bowl. . .
And had a colonic irrigation

I'm the king of the castle
And you're the dirty rascal. . .
I'm a big fat banker
And you're a little customer!

Hickory Dickory Dock
The mouse ran up the clock. . .
The clock struck
And the mouse came out in sympathy

Hush-a-bye baby on the tree top
When the wind blows the cradle will rock
When the bough breaks the cradle will fall. . .
This is a new birthing technique from France

The grand old Duke of York, he had ten thousand men. . .
But then again you know how people talk

There was a crooked man and he walked a crooked mile
He found a crooked sixpence against a crooked stile
He bought a crooked cat which caught a crooked mouse. . .
And they all lived together till he fell off his yacht

Wee Willie Winkie runs through the town
Upstairs and downstairs in his night-gown. . .
In and out of houses and along seaside piers
And when they finally catch him he'll get ten years

Simple Simon. . .
Wore an iPod going to the fair
Said Simple Simon to the pieman: 'What?'

Jack Sprat could eat no fat
His wife could eat no lean
And so between them both you see. . .
They had very little in common

Ladybird, ladybird,
Fly away home
Your house is on fire. . .
And your children have been put in contact
with the local social services

Miss Lucy had a baby
She named it Tiny Tim
She put it in the bathtub
To see if it could swim
It drank up all the water
It ate up all the soap. . .
Where were the bloody social services?

Georgie Porgie
pudding and pie. . .
Went into the gents
Now we all know why

When Susie was a baby, a baby Susie was,
She went: 'Ga, ga, ga-ga-ga'
When Susie was a toddler, a toddler Susie was,
She went: 'Scribble, scribble, scribble-scribble-scribble'
When Susie was a child, a child Susie was,
She went: 'Why? Why? Why-why-why?'
When Susie was a teenager, a teenager Susie was,
She went. . .
Like the clappers

Here we go looby loo,
Here we go looby light
Here we go looby loo. . .
That was a Party Political Broadcast on behalf of UKIP

Not last night but the night before
Twenty-four robbers came a-knocking at the door
I came downstairs for them to see
And this is what they said to me. . .
We're canvassing on behalf of the Conservative Party

Jack and Jill went up the hill
To fetch a pail of water
Jack fell down and broke his crown. . .
And Jill phoned Clumsy Direct, the accident helpline

One potato, two potato,
Three potato, four;
Five potato, six potato. . .
And to follow, Mr Prescott?

Ring-a-ring o' roses
A pocket full of posies,
Atishoo! Atishoo. . .
Catch it. Bin it. Kill it

Ippa dippa dation,
My operation. . .
Ippa dippa duke
D'ya wanna have a look?

Milk, milk, lemonade. . .
Triple vodka – you'll get laid

Jack Sprat could eat no fat
His wife could eat no lean. . .
So she ate in McDonald's
And he in the school canteen

Ip, dip, sky blue
Who's it? Not you!
Not because you're dirty
Not because you're clean. . .
Because I think you're lying
When you say that you're sixteen

Shine up your buttons with Brasso
It's only tuppence a tin. . .
You can also buff up your arso
With a handkerchief soaked in gin

The North Wind doth blow
And we shall have snow
And what will poor Robin do then, poor thing?
He'll sit in the barn
And keep himself warm. . .
And hide from Bill Oddie, poor thing

Diddle diddle dumpling
My son John
Went to bed with his trousers on
One shoe off and one shoe on. . .
Pissed as a fart

Fe Fi Fo Fum. . .
Is Chris Eubank's phone number

Lavender's blue dilly-dilly
Lavender's green
When I am King dilly-dilly. . .
You will be the Duchess of Cornwall

Jargon

Jargon is used in many professions, particularly on the radio in a US election year. At such times the 'Today' programme is replete with jargon, but do you know what it means? Well, when the presenters say: caucuses, primaries, superdelegates, battleground states, electoral colleges, magic numbers, Super Tuesdays, blue states, red states and wedge issues, it means: 'We're all off on a jolly to America for six months to talk bollocks about an event that none of us can influence, but the hotels and expenses are pretty good and I need some duty free.' This is how the teams translated other pieces of jargon.

ESTATE AGENT'S JARGON

No chain involved
The toilet doesn't flush

Ten minutes from the sea
Or even less if the cliff crumbles

Suit elderly couple
Smells of cabbage

A1 condition
The A1 runs through the garden

Under offer
Gazumping in progress

Ideal for first-time buyer
Can only be sold to people who don't know what a real house is supposed to look like

Imposing
The neighbours will come round and never leave

Utility room
A toilet with a washing machine in it

Cloakroom
A toilet that's too small to get a washing machine in it

Bedroom floor finest wood
One heavy footstep and you'll all go down to breakfast together

Ready for immediate occupation
It's in Jersey and the owners were collaborators during the war

Compact garden
Access to window box

Semi-detached
It's falling apart

Indoor WC
Outdoor bath

Ideal for photographer
No windows

Original features
It's an ugly bloke selling it

Green belt
Mouldy skirting

Reduced for quick sale
Someone buy it before it collapses

Built on Victorian lines
They're selling St Pancras

BUILDER'S JARGON

This needs pointing
This needs pointing the other way

We could start Monday
Pick any Monday and you'd be wrong

Make good
Disguise cock-up

A quotation
One eighth of the final price

You'll notice there are a few
differences from the drawings
We had the plans upside down

We're using well-seasoned timber
*We're putting up your new
beam just as soon as the
leaves have dropped off it*

Don't you worry, you won't
know we're there
We won't be there

Oh, we do electrics
No we don't

Pebble dash
*Throw a stone through the
window and run off*

That door won't stick when the
wood's dried out
*That door won't open when the
wood's dried out*

It'll be a feature
It'll be an eyesore

Oh, we do plumbing
No we don't

Dave's off sick
Dave's at one of my other jobs

African Orange would suit this
room
*I've got a whole bucket-load
of it in my van*

DOCTOR'S JARGON

Let's try these new pills
*I haven't the faintest idea
what's wrong with you*

Let's continue with these pills
*I haven't the faintest idea
what's wrong with you*

I'm going to take you off those pills
I've got a very good idea what's wrong with you

You should have come to see me before this
I've got a golf match in twenty minutes

This won't take long
I've got a golf match in twenty minutes

Are you a member of BUPA?
This is going to cost you an arm and a leg (possibly literally)

How are we today?
I'm fine; you look terrible

POLITICIAN'S JARGON

As the Honourable Member is perfectly aware, I have nothing to hide
You bastard, how did you find out?

Honourable Member
Two-faced git

Right Honourable Member
Right two-faced git

Fact-finding mission
Freebie holiday

We're holding an inquiry
Forget it

That is a very good question
That is the only question I actually know the answer to (but I'm still not going to tell you)

All night sitting
I shouldn't have had those oysters

RESTAURANT JARGON

Soup of the day
The day was 14 March 1943

Dawn-picked mushrooms
We don't actually know when Dawn picked the mushrooms

Good evening, sir, my name is André
My name is Neville and I was raised in Catford

Help yourself to as much salad as you like
We have tiny salad plates

Would you like a drink at the bar first?
Your table isn't ready, please give us a lot of money while you're waiting for it

Which wine did you say again, sir?
I'm going to pretend I didn't understand your French accent just to embarrass you in front of your friends

Chef has asked me to say that he particularly recommends the turbot
If we don't shift that turbot by tonight we'll have to throw it out

TRAVEL BROCHURE JARGON

Palm fringed-beach
Surrounded by beggars

Compact swimming pool
Bidet

Sun-drenched
Weather extremely variable

Staggering views
The local wine's dodgy

Demi pension
Half the hotel isn't built yet

We would strongly recommend
hiring a car
*You are 103 miles from the
nearest lavatory*

Plenty of nightlife
Watch out for the cockroaches

Stone's throw from the beach
*Mick Jagger once vomited
from the top balcony*

Name Dropping

Barry Cryer is an inveterate name-dropper, as anyone who's read his memoir will know. It covers the period from the 1950s, when Barry took his first faltering step onto the bottom of the showbiz ladder, right up to early this year, when he thought he'd better try to take another.

Hello Terry.

You won't guess who came round to supper last night.

No idea – you've got a cook, haven't you?

No – we had to SUE COOK. The kitchen utensils were beginning to go missing. Nasty business.

Well, there's nothing worse than a ROBIN COOK. So who made the food?

The kids cooked it on the new Aga. There are so many things the conventional oven can't do that the AGA KHAN. I'm ADAM ANT about it. I just gave the orders: 'JOHN PEEL the potatoes, STEPHEN FRY the onions, PATRICK MOORE salt please,' that sort of thing. I let MIKE REED the recipe from the Delia Smith's 'Summer Collection'. I like THE CRANBERRIES.

I didn't know Michael could read.

He couldn't. But when he was sixteen I told MICHAEL FLATLEY to pull his socks up or I'd boot him up the GARY GLITTER.

KEN RUSSELL?

Oh yes, he's been reading for a while now.

And haven't your Jeremy and *SEAN BEAN* working in Sketchleys?

Yes, Sean operates the tumble dryer and *JEREMY IRONS*. They're a great team.

Well I must say, you and Victoria certainly have a large family. Do you plan to *ROGER MOORE*?

VICTORIA WOOD – but I just don't have the energy these days.

She's a *MINNIE DRIVER*, isn't she?

Oh yes, she loves nippy little cars – not very inclined to *CHER* hers though.

You spoil that woman, you know.

Well, you can't be a skinflint these days – you've got to *SHEIKH YAMANI* about a bit. I bought her *ANNE DIAMOND* necklace for her birthday. Speaking of shopping I'd better get off to the supermarket. *LORD SAINSBURY*'s full on a Saturday afternoon.

TERRY WAITE a minute – you live in South London, don't you? Merton, isn't it?

Not any more – it was a wrench though. My wife *MRS MERTON* dreadfully. And the new house

takes quite a bit of upkeep – we've just had the roof done.

Oh yes?

We had this wonderfully *BONNIE TYLER*. He certainly had his job cut out removing all the lichen.

Lichen?

Oh yes – there was some *STIRLING MOSS* growing up there. Cost me an arm and a leg.

Luckily I'm doing all right now my latest idea has been bought by the Innovations catalogue.

Oh, what is it?

It's something to help the kids keep their Toytown characters tidy. It's called a *NODDY HOLDER*.

BILL ODDIE hell! I wish I'd thought of that.

Chat-Up Lines

'Chat-Up Lines' is a regular favourite and takes as its subject the art of love and romance. Normally the teams don't approve of prising fun out of such a subject. Making love isn't something to be mocked. It's the most tender, beautiful act that money can buy. Here are some chat-up lines to suit certain occupations.

HOSPITAL CHAT-UP LINES

Cough!

Do you coma here often?

My drip or yours?

I hear you're looking for a fine specimen

Got any glasses? I've found a bottle

Did anyone tell you you've got a cute angina?

Your X-rays don't do you justice

Would you like to see what a private room looks like?

Did the bowels move for you?

Is your leg up in plaster or are you just pleased to see me?

PARLIAMENTARY CHAT-UP LINES

Would the Right Honourable lady agree?

Haven't I seen you around the Commons? Which common was it?

I'm Black Rod and I've got the keys to the whip's office

I have an opening for a researcher

I suppose losing my deposit's out of the question?

How would you like to spend an evening with a standing member?

Mind if I poll you?

Ayes to the right, noes to the left – what a pretty face

Get your ermine, you've pulled

ECCLESIASTICAL CHAT-UP LINES

Ha-lo!

Would you care to be de-frocked?

I say, now that's a habit I wouldn't mind getting into

I can think of something I'd like you to alter boy

Hello, would you like to be one of the lay sisterhood?

If anyone can – the canon can

You'll find that I move in mysterious ways

Look, I forgive whatever you're about to do with me

Please kneel, and while you're kneeling. . .

MOTOR MECHANICS' CHAT-UP LINES

I'll just roll you up onto the pavement and then we won't be in anybody's way

What's a nice grille doing in a body like this?

Let's play petrol pumps

Have you been turning this back? You little clock teaser

You'd expect a bit of rattling on one this age

D'you want to put it in first?

I'll give you a jump start and that'll get you going in no time

I'm going to have to get underneath

You realise that this thing is just an extension of my car

DOGS' CHAT-UP LINES

I like your scent. Turn around and let me get a look at your face

Active life isn't all it prolongs

Fancy a bit of 'ruff'?

Fancy doing it human-style?

Since you ask, I _am_ a pointer, but I'm pleased to see you as well

I'll show you my growls if you'll show me your pants

Sit! Lie down! I wish it was always this easy

My aftershave? Oh it's just a little toilet water

I know a great place to eat – honestly, it's the dog's bollocks

Let's paint the town pale yellow

MUSICIANS' CHAT-UP LINES

I suppose a pluck's out of the question?

Just four bars and then let's go back to a flat

Would you care to play with my G string?

This is both grand and upright

Would you like to come Bach to my place?

Wanna go on my organ?

I hope you've got rhythm, because I haven't brought anything

What a funny place to keep a violin. Do you often have a fiddle in your trousers?

I always use a contrapuntal

Duet or solo?

FISHERMEN'S CHAT-UP LINES

Let me show you my tackle

Could you give me a hand? I seem to have got my fly tangled

Would you like to look at my worm?

I think you should know that I've got crabs – in this bucket

Ever seen a ten-foot rod?

You're quite attractive, but you should have seen the one that got away

Don't worry, my dear, I've done this loads of times and I've never caught anything

It may look like a maggot to you but it works for me

Do you want to see the piece of cod that passeth all understanding?

GARDENERS' CHAT-UP LINES

Don't worry – it'll grow

No, no. The green one's the cucumber

D'you think it's better in a bed or up against a wall?

Hiya, Cynth!

'Allo, Vera!

D'you like pansies at all?

I suppose a fork's out of the question?

Could you help me find the clematis?

Come and see the potting shed – first prick out, then harden off

ORNITHOLOGISTS' CHAT-UP LINES

Would you like to come home to my house martin?

I suppose a duck's out of the question?

Personally I think two in the bush is much better than one in the hand

Oh please, put it on my bill

Just put your teeth in the night jar

I say, what a lovely hornbill

How do you like your corncrakes in the morning?

Either I'm using these binoculars wrong or you're a very big boy

'What would you say to twelve finches?'

Don't let a little thrush put you off

One swallow doesn't make a commitment

BUILDERS' CHAT-UP LINES

I hope you don't mind banging

I don't just lay bricks, you know

D'you want to know why they call me Enormous Bill? Because it'll be twice the size of your estimate

Were you thinking of stripping it all off then?

This lot'll have to come down

D'you wanna get felt laid down in the loft?

I'll be in and out within six weeks

Dear oh dear. Who put this in?

It's a hard hat and it's not alone

You won't know I'm here

Mottos

Many organisations or families feel the need to express their guiding principle in a pithy one-liner. Some organisations later regret their choice of motto. When the RSPCA was founded in a tiny office no bigger than a store cupboard, they took the motto: 'Vix fabrefacta feles in hic' (you can hardly swing a cat in here).

Allied Carpets
Fifty Years of Closing-Down Sales

Association of Norfolk Bakers
Two Hundred Years in Bread

The Amputation Society
Go to Work on a Leg

IKEA
I'm Sorry You're Going to Have to Put Your Own Slogan Together

Big Brother
Who Cares Who Wins

The Kamikaze Club
We Missed

British Telecom
Putting You on Hold

The House of Lords
May Contain Nuts

Rabbi Gold Plastic Surgeon
Tips and Wrinkles

Virgin Trains
*This Motto Has Been Withdrawn
Due to It Being the Wrong Kind
of Motto*

Gamblers Anonymous
Bet You Don't Know Who We Are

The Shoemaker's Society
Always Knowingly Under-soled

Hitchcock Trusses
Masters of Suspense

The Literal Society
We Are the Literal Society

The Association of Pedicurists
I Came, I Saw, I Corn Cured

The Jehovah's Witnesses
*When One Door Closes, So Do All
the Others*

The Car Mechanics' Club
Piston Broke? We Can Help

The Famous Jamaican-Italian
Fast Food Drive-Through
Association
Rasta Pasta Fasta

Guild of Plate Glass Shop
Window Removers
We Take Great Panes

The Oxford English Dictionary
Precision Is Our Whatsaname

La Société des Marins Anciens
de la France (Retired French
Mariners)
*To the Sea, It Is the Time (or A
L'eau, C'est L'heure)*

The Anger Management Club
Don't Get Us Started

The Turkey Breeders'
Association
Norfolk and Good

The Federation of Life Support
Machine Manufacturers
*Tubes Help You Breathe More
Easily*

Rod Stewart Ex-Wives' Club
*I Am Not a Number I Am a
Human Being*

The Hampshire Society
Better Safe than Surrey

The Procrastination Society
*One Hundred Years Without a
Motto*

The Tourettes Society
Join Us or F*** Off

Mrs Trellis' Postbag

Whenever a large number of letters shower in on the post-room we can be sure the Scrabble factory's blown up again. And every time we hear the programme's pigeon hole has been crammed to bursting, we know it'll make sitting down rather uncomfortable for the programme's pigeon. Most weeks we know there'll be a letter in there from a Mrs Trellis of North Wales, typical of the many hundreds we receive each week, from Mrs Trellis of North Wales.

Dear Melvyn,
Here's a great tip for removing any annoying little hairs that collect in the bath-plug hole. Tempt them up with a carrot, then pull them out by their long floppy ears.
Yours sincerely,
Mrs Trellis

Dear
Having a lovely
Weather not so
Wish you were
Yours
Mrs
(P.S. Due to power cut in hotel last night, had to write
this under lighthouse)

Dear Mr Cameron,
I saw you on the telly alongside your new chum, Nick.
So that's what they mean by: Conservative with a
little 'C'.
Yours sincerely,
Mrs Trellis,
North Wales

Dear Ulrika
So pleased to hear that Tim Brooke-Taylor is back. With
him away, the show was like Hamlet without the balcony
scene.
Yours sincerely,
Mrs Trellis
North Wales

Dear Miss Toksvig,
Here's one of my favourite cuttings. It's four miles of double track just north of Crewe.
Yours truly,
Mrs Trellis

Dear Mr Titchmarsh,
The liner in my garden pond has developed a leak. Could you please send a lifeboat to get the passengers off?
Yours in haste,
Mrs Trellis,
North Wales

Dear Mrs Antrobus,
Your excellent limerick round has inspired me to try writing one myself, which I would love one day to hear read out loud on the show:
There was a young lady from Slough
Who developed a very bad cough
She wasn't to know
It would last until now
Let's hope the poor girl will get through.
Yours truly,
Mrs Trellis,
North Wales

Dear President Kennedy,
I hear you got shot in Dallas. What is the world coming to? First JR, now you.
Yours sincerely,
Mrs Trellis,
North Wales.

Dear Teams,
When I noticed in the Radio Times that your show was
back, there were three big ticks next to the listing.
So I sprayed them with DDT.
Yours etc,
Mrs Trellis

Dear Kenton,
I was appalled on tuning in this morning to be
bombarded with a torrent of blatant filth. With terms
such as 'large firm', 'holding up well' and 'satisfying
performance' and worst of all 'job blows', it was the
most offensive edition of the Today Programme Business
Report ever.
Yours disgustedly,
Mrs Trellis,
Wild Shag Cottage,
Upper Sheepsbottom Lane
Much Humping on Sea

Dear Shula,
How awful they should have moved the 'Moral Maze' from
its traditional time to be hidden away in some obscure
slot. You can imagine my horror and dismay when I
tuned in specially and found I hadn't missed it yet.
Yours faithfully,
Mrs Trellis, North Wales

Dear Mr Cowell,
I love your 'X Factor'. Best lipstick I've ever used.
Yours sincerely,
Mrs Trellis
North Wales

Dear Bamber,
It's never good policy to store tubes of Superglue and
Vaseline in the same cupboard. If a young wife is in a
hurry, it's all too easy to get them muddled up. I did
once and you can guess what happened. The broken spout
fell straight back off the teapot again.
Yours faithfully,
Mrs Trellis
North Wales

Dear Libby,
Many congratulations to the teams. I've just read the
exciting news that Graeme, Tim and Barry have been
offered long term contracts to appear exclusively on
Sky. And hats off also to the Highlands and Islands
Development Board for giving them the chance!
Yours faithfully,
Mrs Trellis,
North Wales

Dear Mrs Mills-McCartney,
Oh dear. What a mess.
You must be kicking yourself.
Yours as ever,
Mrs Trellis
North Wales

Dear Mr Gadaffi
You must be very proud. It's
not every duck that becomes
president.
Yours in haste,
Mrs Trellis, North Wales

Dear Mr Rees,
I understand you are looking for suggestions for
your Quote Unquote 'programme'. Can you tell me
where the expression 'dull as ditchwater' comes
from?
Yours sincerely,
Mrs Trellis

Dear Mr Titchmarsh
This morning I went out to dig up some dandelions
and a giant hogweed on my lawn. The filthy beast.
Yours faithfully,
Mrs Trellis, North Wales

Dear Mr Ronaldo
You must have been bowled over by your Player
of the Year trophy. Even though it clearly never
touched you.
Kind regards, Mrs Trellis.

Dear Dale,
I tuned into your Supermarket Sweep programme this
morning and was most disappointed to see no sign of
the little fellow. And what's happened to his chum
Sooty?
Yours sincerely, Mrs Trellis

Dear Mr Flintoff,
Well played. Wilma, Betty and Barny must be very
proud of you.
Yubadubadoo, Mrs Trellis.

Dear MoneyBox Live,
I have no mortgage on my house which is worth
£250,000, have about £10,000 savings in a building
society and I receive a generous monthly pension. So
there.
Yours sincerely, Mrs Trellis.

Dear Delia,
While hosting an intimate supper party last night, I
came to thinking I may have misunderstood your recipe
for Ham and Pea soup.
Yours Sincerely,
Mrs Trellis.
PS: Any handy hints for getting vomit stains off
wallpaper?

Dear Dale,
Bet you can't guess who I bumped into at the
optician's the other day.
Thought not. I can't either.
Yours sincerely, Mrs Trellis.

Dear Yoko Ono,
Is it true your name is Japanese for 'One Egg'?
Sayanora for now, Mrs Trellis.
P.S. I swear by your soap powder.

Dear You and Yours,
Look out for cheap torch batteries in Currys. They
play havoc with your dentures.
Yours sincerely, Mrs Trellis.

Dear Angus,
Thanks for the call last night. So sorry I wasn't
available to join you at the Rhyl Motor Lodge for a
can of coke. Despite the bad line, I could just make
out what else you were after, so I've sent along some
friends from the Ladies' Methodist Chapel with a nice
piece of steak. I hope you enjoy your rump with two
Protestants.
Yours sincerely, Mrs Trellis.

Dear David Dickinson,
I can sum up why the BBC have your programme on TV
every night in three words: 'Cheap as Chips'.
Yours etc,
Mrs Trellis.
PS: I can tell by your face that stuff really does do
exactly what it says on the tin.

Dear Mr Tarrant
Is it true that in Japan that you're known as 'Mr Rack
of Tarrant'?
Kind regards,
Mrs Trellis.

Dear Mrs Trellis,
Do you sometimes think you may as well be talking to
yourself?
Yours,
Mrs Trellis

Unclaimed Prizes

All of these fabulous prizes have been available to the lucky winners of our regular Pick Up Song competition. They are impeccably crafted, totally unique and completely unwanted.

This week's prize is guaranteed to accessorise and delight any fashion-conscious pet-lover seeking that classic retro look.
It's this fabulous pair of tortoiseshell tortoises

This week's prize is sure to delight everyone who appreciates jokes being told to match their surroundings.
It's this marvellous stand-up chameleon

This week's prize will ideally suit the sweet-toothed fire-arms enthusiast.
It's this self-loading, semi-automatic trifle

This week's prize will delight any food-loving loan defaulter who wants to put extra flavour into stews or sauces when their house is repossessed.
It's this County Court bay leaf

This week's prize will delight any dog breeder who likes his pets' birthday parties to go with a bang.
It's this handsome tube of canine jelly

This week's prize is sure to delight every atheist DIY enthusiast who likes to use high-quality power tools.
It's this professional cordless secular saw

This week's prize will prove invaluable to anyone considering setting up a vagrant-cleaning business.
It's this commercial tramp steamer

This week's prize is just the thing to delight the budget-conscious pastry chef who wants to be absolutely sure his cakes won't stick to the tin.
It's this helpful greaseproof pauper

This week's prize will delight anyone who enjoys visiting ancient churches, examining commemorative plaques and warmly greeting the churchwardens they encounter along the way.
It's this fine English Heritage arse-rubbing kit

This week's prize will delight any wildlife enthusiast who likes to keep predatory, nocturnal birds warm these cold winter nights.
It's this stylish, heated owl rail

This week's prize will ideally suit the sweet-toothed 'S and M' enthusiast who's always in a hurry.
It's this Bird's Instant Whip

This week's prize will delight every wire-haired terrier owner who likes to keep their pet smartly presented.
It's this lovely Corby Schnauzer Press

This week's prize is certain to eradicate the creeping effect of marine mollusc damage to ageing skin.
It's this Nivea Anti-Winkle Cream

This week's prize is sure to delight every DIY enthusiast who likes to keep their underwear co-ordinated.
It's this selection of Dulux matt emulsion pants

This week's prize is sure to delight every handicraft enthusiast who enjoys making their own Chinese food.
It's this lovely set of knitting noodles

This week's prize is guaranteed to delight any keen gossip-monger who's organising a formal sea-food dinner.
It's this splendid boxed set of vintage fish wives

This week's prize is sure to delight every dinner party host who likes to serve lawn clippings in style.
It's this lovely cut grass decanter

This week's prize is sure to keep anybody's wife warm in bed on a cold winter's night.
It's this electric Blunkett

This week's prize is sure to delight every philatelist with an interest in tree felling.
It's this beautiful, leather-bound stump collection

This week's prize is essential formal wear for your mother's cross-dressing brother.
It's this beautiful uncle-length ball gown

This week's prize will delight any discerning cattle farmer who likes to burn his farmyard waste in luxury style.
It's this solid gold dunghill lighter

This week's prize will prove a boon to anyone who doesn't like to be kept awake at a funeral.
It's this instant de-caffeinated coffin

This week's prize is a refreshing fruit drink that'll make the perfect addition to any packed lunch on school visits to Iraq.
It's this bottle of Sunni Delight

This week's prize is one to be treasured by every member of al-Qaida who's also a fan of the game show 'Three-Two-One'.
It's a life-size Dusty Bin Laden

This week's prize is an ideal snack for the chiropodist on the move.
It's these tasty microwave bunion rings

This week's prize will delight every keen chef who likes their desserts to throw themselves off the cooker.
It's this lovely lemming meringue pie

This week's prize is a satisfying lunch snack that conveniently hangs itself from the ceiling.
It's this tasty pipistrelle bap

This week's prize will ideally suit any home owner who wants to get that authentic inner-city Cardiff effect in their kitchen.
It's this lovely Welsh dosser

This week's prize will delight anyone who suffers from excessively sweaty relatives.
It's this auntie perspirant spray

This week's prize is just the thing to delight the small rodent enthusiast who likes to keep his pets minty fresh.
It's this bottle of Listerine Mouse Wash

This week's prize is guaranteed to give the busy executive a vigorous workout as he sleeps.
It's this luxury double bed with interior-sprung mistress

This week's prize will thrill anyone who likes their woolly hosiery to give long-term satisfaction.
It's these lovely tantric socks

This week's prize is just the thing for the food lover who can never remember what he likes for pudding.
It's this tin of Amnesia Creamed Rice

This week's prize allows even the most inventive of sleepwalkers to wander unencumbered.
It's these state-of-the-art cordless pyjamas

This week's prize is just the thing for the aspiring athlete to keep an unruly carpet in check.
It's this set of anabolic stair-rods

This week's prize is sure to please the French holiday-home owner who needs to clear rabbits from his garden.
It's this cross-Channel ferret

This week's prize comes from the Findus Dermatology Convenience Range.
It's this boil in the bag

This week's prize combines great-looking hair with the exhilaration of the Canadian outdoors.
It's this hair-styling moose

This week's prize will ideally suit the lover of Chinese food who needs to know exactly when it's cooked.
It's this oven-ready speaking duck

This week's prize is just the thing for the DIY reggae enthusiast.
It's this Desmond Dekker workmate

This week's prize will give instant peace of mind to any lover of unusual animals who's worried their pet might go astray.
It's this self-addressed antelope

This week's prize is just the thing to ride around Paris on when doing the Victor Hugo Tour.
It's this economical 1.6-litre hunchback

This week's prize is the ideal break for any floor-covering enthusiast.
It's two weeks on this luxury lino

This week's prize is something so comfortable to sit on, it will make you feel like royalty
It's this Parker-Bowles recliner

This week's prize will ideally suit the dog-loving handyman.
It's this set of adjustable spaniels

This week's prize will delight the sweet-toothed classical music lover.
It's this bag of Schubert Dips

This week's prize will ideally suit the Tibetan hill farmer who likes to keep the place neat and tidy.
It's this matching set of goat hangers

This week's prize is the very latest in transcendental furnishing.
It's an occasional table

This week's prize is sure to delight the sweet-toothed baby Buddhist.
It's this tin of re-incarnation condensed milk

This week's prize comes from the Ann Summers' Erotic Herb Collection.
It's this attractive blow-up dill

Late Arrivals

PART 3

THE VICARS' BALL

Welcome to Mr and Mrs Collar
and their son, Doug Collar

Also here tonight is the Rt Hon.
Charles Ismaeshepherd
*and his father, the Lord
Ismaeshepherd*

Mr and Mrs Nod
and their son, Si Nod

A strange couple from the
church: an abbot and a beadle,
who've formed an unholy
alliance
to produce Beadle's Abbot

It's cabaret time:
*A parade of knickerless
parsons. They're all standing
in a line, they'll get a
queue-rate! Good job I
brought my rev counter.*

Will you also greet
*Benny Dictus, Jenny Fleckt,
Dai O'Sease, Ann Glican-
Church, and on her own –
Penny Tential*

Mr and Mrs Ologist
*and their effeminate bell-
ringing son, Camp Ian Ologist*

Mr and Mrs Meek
*and their saintly son, blessed
Arthur Meek*

Also, Mr and Mrs Ayshon-of-
the-Magi
*and their son, Theodore
Ayshon-of-the-Magi*

Stand and greet Mr and Mrs
Rendeth-the-lesson
*and their son, Andy Rendeth-
the-lesson*

And finally, Mr and Mrs Ment
and their newt, Esther Ment

BUILDERS' BALL

Will you welcome please, Mr and Mrs Cotter-Tiling
and their son, Terry Cotter-Tiling

Will you welcome please, Mr and Mrs Jay
and their daughter, Iris Jay

Mr and Mrs Scleavage
and their daughter, Jean Scleavage

Mr and Mrs Wall-Carpeting
and their son, Walter Wall-Carpeting

Mr and Mrs Back-on-Thursday
and their son, Willoughby

From Ireland – Brendan Beam and James Joist
as well as Con Creet and Mick Ser

Mr and Mrs Lottle-Have-to-Be-Repainted
and their son, Theo Lottle-Have-to-Be-Repainted

The Mendes family
including Rhoda Mendes. . .
she digs having her asphalt

And also from Ireland, Mrs and Mrs O'Doors
and their son, Paddy O'Doors

Mrs and Mrs Antilers
and their son, Rufus Antilers

Mr and Mrs Loadabricks
and their son, Laurie

Mr and Mrs Neepot
and their son, Jim Neepot

Mr and Mrs Chance-of-a-Cuppa-Tea
and their daughter, Henny

Mr and Mrs Duz-Merchants
and their son, Bill Duz-Merchants

Mr and Mrs King-Good
and their daughter, May King-Good

Mr and Mrs Four-Sugars-in-Mine-Love
and their daughter, Olive Four-Sugars-in-Mine-Love

Mr and Mrs Bennett-That's-Twice-the-Estimate
and their son, Gordon

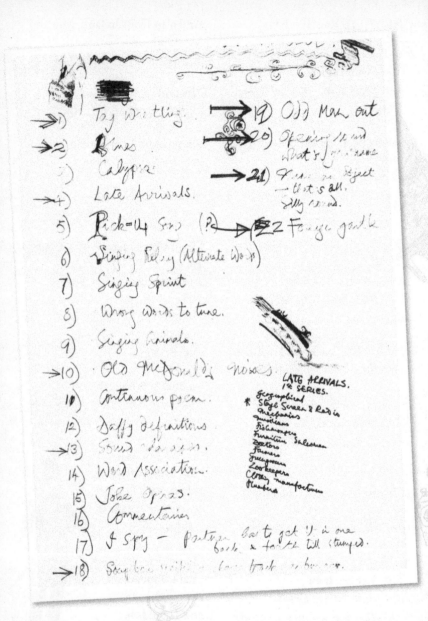

1) Tag Wrestling.
2) Rhymes
3) Calypso
4) Late Arrivals.
5) Pick-up Song (P.) → 22 Foreign gentle.
6) Singing Relay (Alternate Words)
7) Singing Sprint
8) Wrong Words to tune.
9) Singing Animals.
10) Old McDonald's noises.
11) Continuous poem.
12) Daffy definitions
13) Sound design.
14) Word Association.
15) Joke opras.
16) Commentaries
17) I Spy — Picture has to get 'it' in one back & forth till stumped.
18) Soapbox with — has back to home.

19) Odd Man out
20) Opening ?? and what's your name
21) ?? no object — that's all silly ??.

LATE ARRIVALS.
1ª SERIES.
* Geographical
Stage Screen & Radio
Mechanics
Musicians
Fishmongers
Furniture Salesmen
Doctors
Farmers
Greengrocer
Zookeepers
Clergy manufacturer
Plumbers

BRITISH BROADCASTING CORPORATION
AEOLIAN HALL 135-137 NEW BOND STREET LONDON W1Y OED
TELEPHONE 01-580 4468   CABLES: BROADCASTS LONDON PS4
TELEGRAMS: BROADCASTS LONDON TELEX   TELEX: 22182

Ext: 4137/7146

17th November 1971

Dear Graeme,

I thought we were all very unkind to you yesterday, accusing you of letting us in for a dreadful evening. In fact we all survived very adequately, and at least three hundred people seemed to have had an excellent evening's entertainment, so go to the top of the class! I will cut it down to thirty minutes, and I am sure I will be able to sell it as a oncer, and who knows, they may want it on a weekly basis!

Over the next couple of weeks I will try and draw together all the guarantees I have financially to persuade you to do "I'm Sorry". The sum of £800, I am sure, is totally inconceivable, but I think the time has come when we must say what radio's financial effort could be, and if that's not enough, then I think the time will have come to forget it.

Well done to you personally last night, and how right we were about Humph.

Yours,

David Hatch

Graeme Garden Esq.,
16 Farm Avenue,
NW2

IMD

I'M SORRY I HAVEN'T A CLUE

A History

'I'm Sorry I Haven't a Clue' is the most listened-to comedy programme on British radio. It regularly attracts an audience of about 2.5 million on Radio 4, a figure that would put it comfortably into the top ten TV programmes on BBC2 or Channel 4.

The brainchild of Graeme Garden, the programme was devised as an alternative to 'I'm Sorry I'll Read That Again', the chaotic sketch show that ran from 1964 to 1973 starring John Cleese, Graeme Garden, Bill Oddie, Tim Brooke-Taylor, Jo Kendall and David Hatch. Graeme devised a way of turning the show into a game,

which meant not having to write a weekly script and, in 1972, took the idea to David Hatch, at that time a producer in Light Entertainment Radio (later to be Controller of Radio 4 and Managing Director of BBC Network Radio).

Jazz legend Humphrey Lyttelton was the surprise choice for chairman. David Hatch recalled the conversation with Graeme: 'What we already had was a scripted show which was like a composed piece of music and the notion was that we should go off-piste and not have words written down. . . and the equivalent to the composed piece of music was jazz. I think

Radio Times, Tuesday 11 April 1972

12.25 pm *New series*
I'm Sorry I Haven't a Clue
A panel game (?)
starring
Graeme Garden and
Jo Kendall
v
Tim Brooke-Taylor and
Bill Oddie
with Humphrey Lyttelton
in the chair
and DAVE LEE at the piano
Producer DAVID HATCH
(Repeated: Thursday, 6.15 pm)
(Radio Times People: page 4)
12.55 Weather, information and
news for your area

his name emerged over the third pint. I think we both said it together and then both realised how clever we were.'

With no script to rely on, the pilot show, recorded in London's Playhouse Theatre, was a nerve-wracking experience for the cast. When asked in the pub afterwards if he thought that the pilot would ever be broadcast, David Hatch replied that it might go out on Boxing Day, after lunch, when everyone was very drunk. Fortunately, Tony Whitby, then Controller of Radio 4, liked what he heard and commissioned a series of six programmes. The first was broadcast on 11 April 1972 with panellists Graeme Garden, Tim Brooke-Taylor, Bill Oddie and Jo Kendall.

In the first series, Humphrey alternated the chairmanship with Barry Cryer, before making the role his own. One of Jon Naismith's innovations as producer was to bring in a script writer for the introduction and links between rounds. Iain Pattinson has been writing the chairman's gags for the past twenty years.

Comedian and satirist Willie Rushton joined the panel in 1974. He became an entrenched regular and much-loved 'Clue' panellist until his untimely death in December 1996, just two days after recording his final show. Willie's 'off the wall' sense of humour and razor-sharp wit was an essential element in the success of 'Clue'. To this day, nobody has been brought in to replace him on a permanent basis. Over the past few years, Tim Brooke-Taylor has been partnered by a host of talented comedians, including Stephen Fry, Paul Merton, Tony Hawks, Andy Hamilton, Linda Smith,

The cast of I'm Sorry I'll Read That Again

Phill Jupitus, Sandi Toksvig, Ross Noble, Bill Bailey, Rob Brydon, Harry Hill, Jack Dee, Victoria Wood and of course, the show's most regular non-regular – Jeremy Hardy. 'I'm Sorry I Haven't a Clue' can claim to have introduced Jeremy's unique singing voice to an unsuspecting nation.

Many games have featured in the programme over the last thirty years, the most famous of which is 'Mornington Crescent'. The game's rules are notoriously complex and listeners who write in seeking an explanation of the game are usually referred to N.F. Stovold's 'Mornington Crescent: Rules & Origins', now out of print. 'One Song to the Tune of Another' is another favourite round, in which the panellists have to sing the words of one tune to the music of another, accompanied by the show's pianist, Colin Sell. He joined 'Clue' in 1974 and 'soon discovered that accompanying people who can't sing well was part of the joke; I learnt to stop worrying about the microphones, the audience in the theatre and at home, and any sort of personal standards.'

Pneumatic scorer Samantha has been the focus of innuendo for more years than it is polite to mention, ever ready to score just in case points are on offer. There have been two other scorers in the past, 'The Lovely Monica' and 'The Lovely Sven', but it is Samantha who remains the teams' firm favourite.

In its remarkable forty years, the show has picked up virtually every prize for radio comedy going – three coveted Sony Gold Awards, a British Comedy Award for Best Comedy Programme, British Press Guild and Voice of the Viewer & Listener Awards for Best Radio Programme, two Television & Radio Industries Club Awards as Radio Programme of the Year and two Spoken Word awards.

There are sixteen 'I'm Sorry I Haven't a Clue' double audio CDs available from the BBC shop and larger record stores, which altogether have sold over a million copies, making them the best-selling recordings of any radio show still being broadcast today. There are also boxed sets, special editions and 'Live' recordings with the ad-libs goofs and retakes all included. The most recent of these include 'In Search of Mornington Crescent', all three series of 'Hamish and Dougal', the 2007 Christmas show 'Humph in Wonderland' and 'Chairman Humph: A Tribute'.

The 'I'm Sorry I Haven't a Clue' teams have also brought out several books: 'The Official Limerick Collection', comprising the best of the Limerick round; 'The Almost Totally Complete I'm Sorry I Haven't a Clue', featuring edited highlights drawn from thirty years of the show; two best-selling texts devoted to the game that 'ISIHAC' made famous: 'The Little Book of Mornington Crescent', and 'Stovold's Mornington Crescent Almanac 2002'; 'The Uxbridge English Dictionary', and 'The New Uxbridge English Dictionary', a collection of some of the funniest 'new definitions' of words; 'The Doings of Hamish and Dougal: You'll Have Had Your Tea', the collected scripts of the spin-off series of the same name; and 'Lyttelton's Britain' by Iain Pattinson, a collection of Humphrey Lyttelton's observations on the many places visited during fifteen years touring the show.

During the 2008 stage tour, two performances at the Lowry

Producer Jon Naismith explaining the jokes to a distracted Chairman Humph

Centre, Salford, were recorded, and have been edited to form the DVD 'I'm Sorry I Haven't a Clue: Live on Stage'. This is the only complete visual record of the show. Three weeks after the Salford recording, and after thirty-seven years as the programme's chairman, Humphrey Lyttelton died.

The devastating loss of Humph was deeply felt by the fans and everyone involved in the programme, and for a time there were conflicting feelings about the future of the series. The public response was bound to influence any decision, and at first there was a flurry of blogging that the show couldn't possibly continue without Humph at its heart. Then, slowly but surely, thousands of emails started to pour in, begging for 'Clues'' return. This overwhelming response confirmed the decision of the BBC and the show's regulars that 'I'm Sorry I Haven't a Clue'